MARCY BRENNER &
KRISTIN DONNAN

A BAKER'S DAUGHTER

MARCY BRENNER & KRISTIN DONNAN
A BAKER'S DAUGHTER

RECIPES & MEMORIES FROM A FAMILY BAKERY

Copyright ©2019 by Marcy Brenner & Kristin Donnan.
Based on recipes created by Brenner's Bakery, Alexandria, VA

Printed in the United States of America. No part of this book may be used or reproduced in any manner without written permission, except in the case of brief quotations embodied in professional works and reviews. First edition.

Hardcover ISBN: 978-0-9915449-6-7

Book design by Rockin' Dog Studio.
Most photography provided by Brenner Family;
additional photography by Jessie Morrissey and Shane Moore, and Carol Woolgar.
Illustrations by Ginny Foard.
All other image credits noted in Illustration Credits.
Bread sours recipes reprinted with permission from King Arthur's Flour Company.

Published by Marcelle R. Brenner Publishing, LLC
PO Box 734, Ocracoke, NC 27960
marcybrenner@gmail.com

For Max

CONTENTS

PREFACE i

PROLOGUE v

Chapter 1. MILK AND HONEY 1

Chapter 2. BREAD AND WATER 17

    White Bread 38

    Raisin Bread 40

    Rye Bread 42

    Pumpernickel/Rye Marble Loaf 44

    Parker House Dinner Rolls 48

    Bagels 52

    Egg Bread 56

    French Bread 58

    Sour French Bread 60

    Croissants 62

    Oatmeal Bread 66

    Whole Wheat Bread 68

Chapter 3. THE BAKERY 71

    Chocolate Top Cookies 86

    Butter Cookies 90

Chocolate Fudge Icing	92
Sugar Cookies	94
Chocolate Chip Cookies	98
Oatmeal Raisin Cookies	100
Oatmeal Chocolate Chip Cookies	102
Coconut Chocolate Chip Cookies	104
Molasses Cookies	106
Peanut Butter Cookies	110
Gingerbread Cookies	112
Icebox Cookies	114
Fruit Bars	116
Chapter 4. THE WHISTLER	**119**
Yellow Pound Cake	132
Chocolate Pound Cake	134
French Pound Cake	135
Angel Food Cake	136
Yellow Layer Cake	138
Seven-Layer Cake	140
Icing	142

Chapter 5. MISS CHARLOTTE	145
Vanilla Custard	168
Pie Crust	170
Pumpkin Pie	172
Pecan Pie	174
Coconut Custard Pie	176
Coconut Macaroons	178
Danish Pastry	180
Doughnuts	186
Pecan Sticky Buns & Loaf	192
Biscuits	196
Chapter 6. SISTERS	199
Brownies	218
Apple Cinnamon Nut Loaf	222
Chocolate Éclairs	224
Boston Cream Pie	228
Petit Fours	230
Gingerbread Cake	232
Radio Bars	234

EPILOGUE	237
ACKNOWLEDGMENTS	245
APPENDIX. BAKING NOTES	251
Bread Sours	278
ILLUSTRATION CREDITS	287
ABOUT THE AUTHORS	288

PREFACE

It was the fall of 1977 in the temperate, sticky forest of suburban Virginia. One of us was raised in this lush, humid, Southern-tinged place; the other came from the Great Plains, unused to sidewalks and buses and people with accents. One of us was tall and lithe, a girl who wore sports uniforms in the school's colors. The other was not a "joiner," and relied on skills that were not as evident from the outside.

One of us still has a preternatural memory, an ability to recall events from when she was a baby—or even when she was a teenager. The other relies on accounts from her friends, because her "memory" exists as sensory flashes. Feelings. Scents.

When we met, Marcy was a Freshman and Kristin—"Krissy" at the time—was a Sophomore. Marcy says we met in Ms. Forman's English class, and that Ms. Forman's was the first classroom on the left, past the "Jock Rail" where the cool kids hung out. She says we were instant friends, and that Krissy was not put off by her stories—her stories of unusual life experiences, her teenage version of herself.

This is most likely all true, although Krissy has no idea where Ms. Forman's classroom was. She does know that we teenagers became friends because both of us operated at face value. Sometimes shockingly so. Marcy's family life—the one portrayed in this volume—set the stage for their friendship.

This book tells the story of Brenner's Bakery, which formed the "rye starter" of Marcy's world. The bakery, which was an extension of her father, Max, was the cornerstone for Marcy's "people"—her family and friends, and their significant moments. In later life, the bakery remained the source of proof that events were real, that life was changing. A birthday or wedding didn't exist without Max's cake. A vacation wasn't legitimate without Danishes. A Relay for Life wasn't complete without Chocolate Tops.

Marcy has been talking for years about resurrecting the recipes that Max used—and that other Brenners created before him. She has been baking and testing, organizing and recalling, taking notes and running ideas, and filling in gaps thanks to relatives and retired bakery staff. Past customers and fans have come out of the woodwork, and out of Facebook, to tell their stories. And Max, toward the end of his life, provided precious first-hand knowledge and memories.

And then she started writing. Marcy is a songwriter—and now a self-taught baker. She's a storyteller who uses words and hands to make sense of things. And sometimes her lyrical thoughts need a corral, or a daisy chain, or context to tie them together. She asked her old friend—a writer and editor—for a look-see. Something interesting happened. We found that when one person knows another person this well, sometimes she can read her mind. Sometimes she can read between her words, recall how she felt during important moments, and relive the past with her. Sometimes she acts as a witness or a devil's advocate. Sometimes she says, "Please, more of that," or "Eh, not so much there." And when people are this close, they speak their truths and trust each other. And the work improves.

In the process, it was easy to maintain Marcy's voice, a voice Krissy has had in her in head for most of her life. The story is presented in the way Marcy tells it.

In this collaborative process of stitching together their shared experiences, these two friends melded their decades of experience. Together, they constructed the story of this singular, sweetest-man-in-the-world father, and of his wife, his daughters, his bakery. Part memoir and part cookbook, *A Baker's Daughter* keeps alive the one man universally loved by everyone we knew.

He was the man who saw us just like we were: a little salt, a little honey. He scooted over and made room for us. He cranked the engine and took us on another spin. He never asked too many probing questions.

And no matter what he might have caught us in, he just smiled, shook his head, and whistled. "You two are hell," he said.

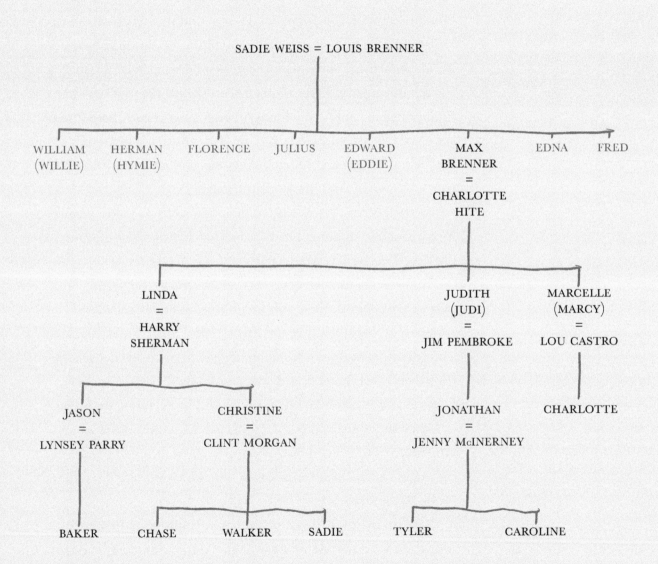

PROLOGUE

Although prologues are usually placed only in fiction books ("In a galaxy far, far away...") the general timeline of the ancestral Brenner family provides the launching pad for my understanding of my father—and, perhaps, myself. It illustrates the history of baking in the family, and sets the stage for the bakery that became the centerpiece of my family's world.

My intent for this book was not to research the complete genealogy of my family, nor was it to document in great detail all of the Brenner's Bakeries' history. My main focus has always been to recreate the recipes for kitchen use. My version of this history will be incomplete and imperfect—and like any living document, will evolve. If any reader has information to make my account more accurate, please let me know and I'll update it. Same goes for recipes. Please send feedback so I can edit them as needed, so they'll be the best version of themselves.

New York, New York—1917. My grandfather Louis marries Sadie Weiss; their first son, William, is born there. As the story goes, they left to avoid epidemics sweeping the city.

The people who knew the details of this history have passed away, but with help from family and news reports, I was able to cobble together at least a rough timeline. However, some early bakery/move dates are approximate; birth dates are accurate. The quoted lines are reflections from my dad about his siblings.

Above: Florence and Rose, 1942
Opposite page: Top: Dad and Edna, 1938. Bottom: Fred, 1960s or 1970s.

Norfolk, Virginia—1918. Louis works at a Greek bakery, then at his Uncle Joe's bakery—and then he opens his own bakery. He and Sadie have two more boys in Norfolk, Hymie (1919) and Julius (1920). Dad on these brothers: "Hymie was a fun-loving, good-time, story-telling, and exaggerating bull-jiver—who took me to my first big league baseball game. Julius was the sweetest and best man I ever knew, and a lover of everyone and everything that was genuine. He joined the Navy as a gunner and photographer in aircraft carrier fighter planes."

Petersburg, Virginia ≈1922. Louis opens a new bakery; son Eddie (1922), and daughters Florence (1923) and Rose (1926) are born. "Eddie was a perfectionist, it had to be his way. He was intelligent about how things worked, but not so good about how people worked. My oldest sister, Florence, was beautiful, always soft spoken, and determined. She worked as a government secretary and also helped in the bakery on weekends. Sister Rose was a knock-out looker who was quick-witted and tough. She taught me to dance, and also worked for the government."

Roanoke, Virginia ≈1927 or 1928. At another new bakery, my father Max (1928) and Edna (1930) were born. "My sweet little sister Edna was a darling, whom I cherished. She was ill most of her life, but always had a wonderful smile and pleasant persona. She was a wonderful sister, wife, and mother."

A BAKER'S DAUGHTER

Washington, DC ≈1931. Louis moved the family north to find work, but the Great Depression made it difficult. Sadie and the children stayed behind while Louis then went to Seattle to work with brother Abe. After he returned, he opened a bakery at 807 4th Street in SW Washington, DC, in 1933. The family lived on the floors above the bakery, where the last child, Fred (1935), was born. He was the only sibling still living when Dad was telling me these stories. "Brother Fred is one of a kind. A brilliant mind, he could do anything he wanted. We worked together in the bakery for a while, and he was a good baseball pitcher as a young man. He started out as a musician, going to the Eastman School of Music and Juilliard, but gave it up. He studied finance, languages, was a stock broker, a racetrack handicapper, writer, and is a gambler at heart."

In 1939, the impacts of World War II caused the 4th Street bakery to close, and Louis took a job at a commercial bakery.

Arlington, Virginia—1946. Louis and son Hymie, together with sons / returning soldiers Julius and Eddie, open a bakery on Columbia Pike. Sons Willie and Max are employees. It is a great milestone for the family.

Post-war era: The Arlington bakery expands to five outlets. Max's brother Hymie eventually takes over the original Arlington bakery, which moves in 1965 down Columbia Pike to the

PROLOGUE

Above: Julius as a WWII naval pilot.
Opposite page: Seated, from left: Willie and Big Bubbe. Standing: Fred, Eddie, Dad, and Julius. Maybe Hymie was taking the photo. 1950s.

Westmont Shopping Center, at the intersection of South Glebe Road. The bakery is sold in 1976 to two employees, who will run that location until it finally closes in 2001.

After Willie goes off to experience life, he returns—as the Brenners always do—to bake. He and Max buy the Belle View Shopping Center branch bakery in 1953, which is located south of Alexandria between Mount Vernon Parkway and Fort Hunt Road; they partner there for twenty-five years. "My oldest brother was a very kind, powerful man," Dad recalls. "He boxed some, and as a young man, he went to work in a CCC camp, building Skyline Drive in Shenandoah National Park."

Moving on: When Max retires in the mid 1980s, his son-in-law Harry Sherman, who had worked with him for many years, continues to operate the Alexandria bakery until the mid-2000s. Our Brenner's location would operate for more than 50 years.

Meanwhile, the first Five Guys hamburger location opens in the Arlington Westmont Shopping Center, just down from the original bakery's second location. As Five Guys gears up to franchise, it needs extra ovens to keep up with its increased hamburger bun demand. Generously, Brenner's shares its kitchen space with Five Guys—after hours, at no charge.

Then, after our Alexandria location closes, Harry becomes the bakery quality-control manager for Five Guys, traveling to the various Five Guys bakery locations to ensure that the buns

are produced to standards. To this day, he remains a Five Guys bakery consultant.

The Westover branch sells to Sansbury Sweeney, a cake decorator, who later develops "The World's Best Cheesecake." And, in 2011, Markos Panas opens a lovely specialty café and bakery—Bread & Water Company—at our old family location. As this book reveals, that name will have an enduring impact on me.

PROLOGUE

ZIS TATE
SUGAR DADDY

CHAPTER 1
MILK AND HONEY

"What's the first memory you have of *your* Dad's bakery?" I ask my father. We're sitting at his sunny kitchen table in central North Carolina, and I'm filled with wistful, romantic thoughts of what his memories surely will reveal. Maybe how he trundled down from their apartment upstairs to his favorite spot, next to his father or one of his older brothers. Maybe when he shaped dough for the first time. Maybe how he could barely reach the wooden counter, or when he snuck a just-baked cookie or a nip of icing.

But he doesn't remember the "first time," because the bakery just was. It wasn't full of sugar and spice and friends from school. "It was just work for me, baby," he says. The layers of meaning in that simple sentence filter across his face—and fall like dominoes inside me.

There have been a few moments in my life when I grew up, and this is one of them. I understand that the bakery was a way of life, a member of the family. In an instant, all those decades later, I feel in my gut that the bakery defined us all, and that even in its absence, it remains the heart of our family. The bakery still tells his story, their story, our story. The bakery, I see now, was my father's life's work—and my family's destiny.

I don't confess that my heart just fell a notch when I sensed how different our experiences have been. Or that with one sentence, my joy—my heart center—just morphed into my father's labor. And my father morphed from my daddy into a man, a worker, a businessman, and a provider.

The bakery was his fate, just like his father's had been in Poland. It was a given that he and his brothers would enter into the family business. "I was about nine when Pop stood me on that wooden box next to the bakery work bench and taught me to make bread," Dad recalls. "I thought I was on top of the world, a big man."

In contrast, my first memories of the bakery—another bakery, the one I grew up in—are sensory: smells, tastes, textures, and sounds. Each night, Dad came home with dried chunks of sugar and dough down the front of his white T-shirt and pants. The family dog would lick his shoes clean every night. The bakery came home to me as a sweet, doughy daddy and lots of bread and goodies. I tell him that. He ponders in the way he would ponder, taking his time, no rush.

"No," he shakes his head slowly. "I can't recall a first memory of the bakery. It just was. It's what we did," he says. "We didn't make anything sweet."

"Nothing sweet?!" I'm floored. He smiles. He knows exactly what case we went for, from the first moment we were old enough to reach into the cases.

"We only made bread and rolls, recipes from the Old Country. Pop was a bread baker, there were no sweet things. He'd make the dough, proof it overnight, and we'd bake it off in the morning. That was our work." He describes the process with no sense of nostalgia. He is not wistful; the memories are not romantic.

Previous page: Max having a cookie in the bakery, near the iconic swinging doors with the round windows.

Above: Max in the midst of one of his specialty tasks: decorating a wedding cake.

MILK AND HONEY

"Pop would work on bread at night. Willie's work was carried out in the day-bakery, where the sweet stuff was made," he explains. "Willie came up with all the sweet recipes." Willie was his eldest brother, much older than Dad, and Willie knew the ropes by the time Dad joined the team. Still, I'm surprised at how Dad describes him. "He was a very nice and polite man, and he helped greatly to make Brenner's Bakery a good business." This sounds a bit like a résumé, or an obituary, and it underscores the idea that they were workmates first. Colleagues.

Well, they were bakers.

As a baker's daughter, I had fresh brownies, the icing still soft, any time I wanted them. Doughnuts on Sunday. And no Wonder Bread in the house. I brought Dad to show-and-tell at school, where he wrote all my classmates' names in icing on their cupcakes. Each year, I could choose any type and decoration I wanted for my birthday cake. All year, I could eat (almost) as much raw dough as I wanted. For my two older sisters and me, being daughters of a baker was a jubilee, a dream come true, and every bit the fascination. The bakery was a second home. A rivalrous sibling. A jealous mistress. A bright sparkling oasis of delights. And the keeper of the family story.

No one could open the front doors of the bakery and not break into a grin when hit with the aroma of sugar and yeast. For customers, it was a place of happiness, nourishment, celebration, and community. For those who worked with my dad, it was a good job working for a dear man. For my friends, it was baked goods after school and "Mr. Brenner" as the cupcake-with-sprinkles in their lives, standing for hours in the shallow end of the community pool, so we girls could swim through his legs and dive off his shoulders. For this baker's daughter, the bakery was magic, a lot of work from time to time—and is probably the reason why I had so many friends.

All of my stories birth from that hallowed place. The bakery is at the heart of every family story. The soundtrack was Dad's ever-present whistling—in the back at the ovens, around the work stations, down in the basement, slipping into a display case alongside each pastel tray filled with fresh product. I can still feel the cut of the white string as it sliced into the crook of my pinkie. We pulled that white string from shiny brass tubes, one mounted at each end of the two front pastry cases. We wrapped it around the precious white boxes—two loops, then a 90-degree spin, then twice around again, then a bow. Being able to tie boxes was a distinct rite of passage. Until I developed a callous, my pinkie bled on the string, and I would have to start again. If you used scissors, well, no one would say it out loud, but you were a sissy.

I can still feel my childish anticipation of my own future wedding day, when I'd look at the cake tops in the rounded glass and wood corner displays—wedding brides and grooms. The bride in her white lace gown, the groom in his black-and-white tuxedo. There was no other skin color than pink or any pairs

of women or men, but you could order them. I saw them in the catalog. I dreamed about my wedding cake, and how many tiers it would have, and the actual, functioning champagne fountain that could sit on top. I would need a very large cake for that. I saw it in one of the wedding cake picture books.

I still hear the sound of Dad's crotchety brown-and-tan adding machine, calculating bills and payroll with its slot-machine handle that, every Monday night, came down with a crunching jangle of buttons. The bakery woke us up in the morning and sang us to sleep at night. We stopped in before we left town, and on the way back. Every time. Like a child, it required constant care, feeding, massaging, attending. Like an aging parent.

My family, friends, and neighbors have their own memories and stories of the bakery—or their branch of the family and another Brenner's Bakery. Or another, as there were several Brenner's Bakeries in three states. Like the generation before them, Dad and his eight siblings all believed in making family around work. It was both impossible and unnecessary to identify whether they were first brothers or bakers; it was all one thing.

Stirring life and work together had begun with their parents, who had come from Eastern Europe to "Amerika," escaping Jewish persecution, seeking the land of milk and honey. The kids learned baking from their father and family from their mother—my Bubbe, Sadie Weiss Brenner. To her, making food for others was serving love.

A BAKER'S DAUGHTER

All these years later, Max's legacy still does the Brenners proud. He personified milk and honey, served love in his mother's image. This is his story. Well, this is *my* story of *his* bakery, the Max Brenner bakery—Brenner's Bakery in Alexandria, Virginia. And this is the story he told me about his family and how that family came to create the center of my universe.

But, to be fair, it's not just my universe.

On the *Brenner's Bakery Memories* Facebook page, memories of Dad and the bakery are tended by hundreds of members. Snapshots of birthday and wedding cakes, stories about the blizzard of '66 when dad brought neighbors bread and pies. And mostly, remembrances of what Max's love felt like, what a gift he gave us all. This community considers the bakery a member of their families, too, and I shared the entire feed with Dad. He wept. Although he built this loving community, he did it merely by making delicious foods, and being his heartful self.

He had no idea what the bakery has meant to all of us until he read those Facebook remarks. "I never thought that bakery would ever bring a tear to my eye," he whispered. He reread the posts from neighbors, past employees, and cousins; he was reminded of everyone's favorite bakery goodie, and of course, how no one could have a holiday without Brenner's.

It's no surprise that these stories—our collective experiences—do not focus on the food. They vibrate to the resonance of the bakery's center. They vibrate to Max.

Opposite page: A sketch of my childhood "dream wedding cake," with a functional champagne fountain; these exist!

Above: Max looking pretty grown up, age 10, 1938.

MILK AND HONEY

BAKING MEMORIES TO LIFE

The two main ingredients in bread are water and flour—but you can't make leavened bread without yeast. Bread will be ruined if the water is too hot, which kills the yeast, or too cold, which leaves it inactivated. I didn't understand the subtleties of this balance when I first started baking bread. Before yeast imbued my house with its universe of pungent aromas, my kitchen was dead; my hands were ignorant. But the more bread I baked, the livelier my kitchen became. The yeast reminded my hands of how to let it run through my fingers, how to invite it into a burst of warmth.

And whether I was baking bread or sweet foods, I quickly learned that baking is a combination of exactitude and intuition, feel and experience. To bake special recipes, it's best to add a pinch of magic. Fairy dust. Sprinkles.

Ever since I left home at eighteen, I have longed to be able to make the bakery's recipes in my own kitchen. Now and then, I would think about what that would require. In my mind's eye, I could still see the "recipes." They were a professional kitchen's version of records, index cards with ingredients lists written in my father's hand. They were tucked into the bookcase in his office nook, next to his desk. He'd reach for them, past the stack of receipts and invoices, jotted notes and keepsakes, all held down by a rock I'd given him for Father's Day. It was painted in kindergarten silver, and glued with glitter and shiny stars. My sister Linda had transcribed some of the recipes, and several of the original cards still existed. Once I got serious, my brother-in-law Harry Sherman sent them to me. He'd taken over the bakery, and inherited its history.

Dad and I started working together on paring down recipes to kitchen-size, step-by-step methods. And then there came a day when he simply tried to explain his process. Through the fog of early dementia, he carefully outlined calculations on a sample page of recipes, and told me that I was now to carry this project forward without him. So I started baking.

Although I have dreamed the dream, and seen the machine in motion, I've never been a professional baker. I quickly discovered that those lists of ingredients, even coupled with Dad's general

> January 23, 2012
>
> Dear Marcy,
> This is the only copy of the Brenner's Bakery Cookies! It will take some work to break it down to HOME BAKING!
> I am sure you can do it!!
>
> Love your Dad

instructions, were not the same thing as having an experienced baker write a proper recipe. I did my best to put myself in his shoes, ratchet down huge, commercial-bakery ingredients and quantities to kitchen-size, then translate them to grocery-store ingredients. I had to trust the freshly scribed recipes, remember (and ask) how to finish, experiment, guess, test, taste, write, and revise the recipes. And then test them again, several times, in fact, until they came out just like the bakery's. Or at least my memory of them.

I apprenticed myself as a bread baker, learning to make the sour starter and rye sour from scratch, making bread every day until I got the hang of it. I ate way too much raw dough, of course. I love raw dough. The smell as it mixes and bakes, a warm bite right out of the oven, a taste the next day—it all brought me back to the bakery in a deep, olfactory way. It sometimes literally made my knees weak with longing. I found myself alone in the kitchen, a big grin plastered on my face. I would go outside just to come back in, so I could smell it fresh again.

I also began to experience a host of both sweet and savory sense memories. I saw my youthful self at the bakery, school clothes covered by an apron, my hair in braids, my hands plunged into a mound of raw dough. I felt the sensation of my father's hands on my youthful ones, as he tried to teach me how to read the gluten fibers, to feel the air pockets, to shape the dough into a roll, or into a pastry. I saw the flutes of frosting tracing the edge of a wedding cake. I smelled the grease cooling in the fryer from the morning's doughnuts, the cinnamon and sugar powder hanging in the air. Yeast. The cigarette smoke curling around dad's face as he waited by the oven.

Over one winter, I made a bread and a sweet item every day. As I walked around the house, I found myself scraping bits of dough off my shirt with my fingernails. I brushed under my nails every night. By the end of the winter, I was wearing Dad's apron when I baked. I still do.

I also knew what recipes I was going to replicate.

WHAT'S INCLUDED, OR NOT

To choose the best, reproducible recipe collection—one that would honor both my dad's legacy and his ancestors' legacy—I began with the bakery's "fan favorites." Then, I added my own favorites and special treats that my family members loved. Then, I sprinkled the recipes throughout the story of our generations.

The recipes also naturally fell into logistical categories. On one hand, when a "favorite" recipe had a hand-written bakery card, I did everything I could to rediscover it and record the result as fully as possible. On the other hand, some recipes didn't have cards. If I really needed them, usually I could figure them out. For example, you'll find Apple Cinnamon Nut Loaf, Bostom Cream Pie, Cinnamon Swirls, French Pound Cake, Pecan Sandies, Petit Fours, Radio Bars, Seven-Layer Cake, and Vanilla Custard.

If you're looking for a specific Brenner's recipe that isn't in the book, then please write and ask, just in case. I might have a card for it, but didn't recreate the recipe. It's never too late to ask.

Of course, some recipes eluded me, or just didn't make the cut. And finally, there was a small list that I was unable to make for technical reasons. In the spirit of full disclosure, some of these details appear below.

GONE BUT NOT FORGOTTEN

Some of my favorite recipes involved "special circumstances" that prevented my recreating them. I will forever miss them:

Recipes Made From Mixes or a Base
Chocolate (Devil's Food) Layer Cake and Cheesecake were made from mixes, so they are not included here. For the record, the cheesecake was made from a product called "World's Best Cheesecake" (and it was).

As for Hard Rolls, they were made from a base, which likewise took them out of the running. In my research, I learned that Kaiser rolls, salt sticks, and poppy seed rolls all were made from the same hard-roll dough base. Although they were the bomb, I felt it best to leave them out.

Hamburger and Hot Dog Rolls
The famous hamburger joint Five Guys used the Brenner's recipe to develop their rolls, and now they own this recipe. I cannot publish it, but you can sure enjoy those rolls at Five Guys.

Max at my second wedding, in 1993, after finishing the cake set-up. His job was done, his flower was pinned—and his heart was open, as it always was.

MILK AND HONEY

By the time I was ready to begin the book, I felt like a different person. I felt like I was "more of a Brenner," and I was seeing the world differently. Everywhere I looked, I saw vast corporations, and shops with distant headquarters. Convenience, cookie-cutter. In contrast, the more I baked, the more Brenner's Bakery represented a sepia moment, a time of butchers, bakers, and specialty stores. Its past customers still ache with nostalgia, yearn for the familiar, remember belonging to a community. Our people used to know and take care of one another. We had block parties, fireworks on the baseball field, and lemonade stands.

And on every day except Monday, you could buy a warm loaf of bread and a box of sweets at Brenner's. If you were lucky, as you reached for your familiar white box, you might catch a glimpse of the man himself. Max might be sliding another tray of goodies into the case, his blue eyes sparkling, his trademark smile lighting his face. You might hear the whistle—or even a few words—before he was gone again, through the swinging doors. Unless there was a child in the bakery line. Then he might ask, "You don't like cookies, do you?" And he would hand one over.

I always associated Dad's silky, lyrical drawl with the sound of Southern musicians. When I closed my eyes, his voice sounded like a Black jazz or blues player's. Someone introducing a song. "Hope you like this one, Baby. I wrote it just for you."

I conjure his voice when I sit in my writing room, overlooking the harbor, with the sun reflecting off Silver Lake and projecting little waves of light that dance on the walls. I know that the bakery—the physical space, the building that smelled a certain way and looked a certain way and felt a certain way—now only lives on in our memories, but I'd like to go there one more time.

Unlike my dad, I do have a first memory: the loud clanging of the big ring of keys as they circled around, banging against the metal and glass, when he unlocked the front door to the bakery. Those keys released the cinnamon-sweet, fruity, almost beer-infused aroma that never changed, throughout my whole growing up. This is what I think of when I'm right over there—in my kitchen—as I bake.

This is what I think of when I'm baking memories of the sweetest man this world has ever known. When I'm baking my extraordinary father back to life.

CHAPTER 2
BREAD AND WATER

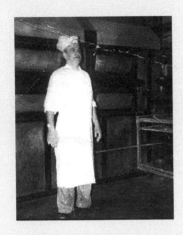

There's a melancholy that weeps in my cells when I imagine Louis Brenner making only bread, nothing sweet. My grandfather was about the basics. No nonsense. A crust outside with a soft center, like a hard roll. Big Bubbe, or Pop, as everyone else called him, was a living demonstration of a simple philosophy of what it took to live. Basic food, religion, and community. He arrived in America with a heart filled with Jewish tradition and ritual. And a pocketful of recipes.

In my life, I've gotten down to meager provisions in only a few instances. Each time, bread was a staple, sometimes the only staple. I packed it when snow camping in the Sierras, relied on it when I was fighting cancer, and lived on it after my little girl died, when my body simply shut down. I reflect that my doomed ancestors were given bread and water, if anything, before they were murdered for being Jewish. In none of those occasions was a cookie or cake on the menu. What I think of as sweet is associated with celebration. Conversely, I see bread as biblical, for "going to the desert," and it's also communion. It's a basic ingredient for survival—family, shelter, food. Big Bubbe was bread and water.

My grandfather came to America from Mielec, Poland, sailing from Hamburg, Germany, in 1913. I saw his name on the ship's record at the National Archives. He was nineteen and had been an apprentice baker since he was seven. His brothers Israel and Abe had come before him to work with their Uncle Max, who came to America in 1881. By the end of the First World War,

"Bread is the staple of life. Bread starts it all."
~ *Louis Brenner*

A BAKER'S DAUGHTER

no one else from Louis's family remained in Eastern Europe—excepting, as the story goes, one male relative who had barely survived a concentration camp. He was broken in every way, and although he wrote for help, there was nothing anyone could do for him. He was never heard from again. Like so many others, our family tree has branches that simply end, relatives who were lost in the Holocaust.

Louis landed in New York, where he rented a garage with an oven. He lived from hand to mouth, buying a bag of flour a day, baking bread at night, and selling it from a basket in town. Eventually, he went to a Greek bakery looking for work. The owner knew a little German and asked, "How would you make this rye bread?" When Big Bubbe answered—correctly, and in German—he was hired. He started the next day.

As Uncle Freddie told it, Big Bubbe worked hard his whole life. Since he apprenticed so young, he was a solid baker by the age of fifteen. He worked at night, seven days a week. He carried that deliberate, signature approach into his marriage to my grandmother, Bubbe, and into the parenting of their six sons and three daughters.

All of the sons were bakers—except for Fred, who was a musician, Buddhist teacher, linguist, author, and professional gambler. Dad told me that everyone in the family wished that Fred had focused on music; everyone else was married to baking, and it made them lighter on their feet with the idea that one

Opposite page: Louis Brenner, Max's dad—and "Pop," or "Big Bubbe" to the rest of us—next to the big ovens in his bakery. **Above:** The Brenner siblings, early 1930s. On the horse, from left to right: Florence, Max, Julius; standing, Hymie and Willie.

Uncle Freddie taking his solo with fellow jazz cats from Juilliard, New York City, circa 1955.

of them was creative. The only place Big Bubbe allowed for creativity, or softness, or indulgence, was with his grandchildren.

As Dad told it, "My Dad, Louis, was tough on the outside but a real softy on the inside. He was as stubborn as a mule, but would listen to your version of an incident, if only for a moment, and then tell you how stupid you were. He loved us in his way—not by saying so, but by actions and words that your mind understood as well as your heart. He had diabetes, but would not learn to give himself insulin shots. Mom would have to give them, and he swore she was getting even with him for all the mean things he said to her in their lifetime together. He suffered inwardly and outwardly when one of us got sick or hurt. I remember when Hymie and I were lost in a boat on Chesapeake Bay overnight. He thought we were dead. After we were rescued and came home, he stayed in bed for two days, getting over his emotions. He died after losing both legs and growing weak in other vital organs. The last time he smiled was when I took you to visit him in a convalescent home. You were three years old and called out 'Big Bubbe!' while peeping through the rails beside his bed. He smiled and rubbed your hair and said, 'Hello!' He never spoke again. I cried uncontrollably at his funeral. I loved him very much. He was a good man."

Babies transformed Big Bubbe. Maybe because they provided a space where he could put aside the ache of his family's sorrows and the relentless struggles of his life in this new country.

A BAKER'S DAUGHTER

His grandchildren brought joy, momentarily erasing the pressures of his life, maybe even pushing away some demons. With us, he shrugged out of his tough cape, and all we knew was his unguarded warmth. It reminded me of when you open an oven door and are blasted by a rush of heat. When I was older, I wondered if he tied his own children to the emigration—the pain of loss—while we were the Holocaust's inevitable phoenix. Or maybe he could let down his guard simply because he didn't feel so responsible for our survival. Whatever his reasons, I loved it.

"He sure loved babies," dad said, all wispy sounding.

Big Bubbe in a moment of reflection, circa 1930s.

BREAD AND WATER

Sadie Weiss Brenner, Max's mom and my Bubbe, as a recent immigrant in New York, circa 1915.

My grandmother Sadie Weiss Brenner was born in Ungvar, Ukraine. Her father, Abraham, was a butcher who raised and butchered animals in a small barnyard at their home. When Sadie was ten, her father went to the hospital seeking treatment for a deep cut and was told, "Jews complain about every little thing, come back tomorrow." He died of gangrene that night. The remaining family moved to Budapest, which had two sides, Buda and Pest. My grandmother—sometimes Little Bubbe, and sometimes just Bubbe—told my Uncle Freddie that one side was

A BAKER'S DAUGHTER

poor and the other affluent. Her mother, Pauline, would buy eggs in the poor part and sell them in the rich part for a little profit.

Bubbe came to America in 1915, when she was only fifteen, thanks to her brother, David. He had immigrated a few years before, settled in Detroit, and then sent her the money to follow him. The family has told and retold her story about traveling in the bottom of the ship, during a rough crossing. The food was terrible, and she became terribly sea sick. My dad and I inherited that sensitive stomach from her. I can imagine how utterly alone she felt on the journey, depleted, spent, afraid.

When she arrived in New York, she found a job as a seamstress in a dress-making factory, what we would call a sweat shop. But her next posting showed her another side of the city—she landed a job taking care of a wealthy family, living on Park Avenue in a fancy house. She was treated well, and saved enough money to help David send for their mother after the war. By then, Pauline's second husband also had died, and she was alone again.

A cousin shared a copy of a handwritten page on which Bubbe wrote a short biography. Whenever I read it, I hear her accent, the lilt of her voice in my head. I feel a mixture of strength and terror and empathy—but I'm not sure which feelings are hers, and which are mine. The words themselves are rather plain. Stark. But they express an uncompromising reality. I know without doubt that this girl could so easily have slipped away. Selling eggs one day, gone the next.

A short, handwritten biographical sketch, written by Bubbe for her children.

"Born in Hungary in a city called Ungwar. I had 4 brothers. We were very poor. We lived in one room and a wood stove. My mother worked very hard. She had to go to the woods and chop wood to keep children warm. Then we couldn't pay our rent so the owner took the little stove out and we had no heat and mom couldn't fix our food so my 3 little brothers caught cold and died. My oldest brother and I lived. My brother David came

A BAKER'S DAUGHTER

to America and when I was 15 he sent for me just before the first (world) war broke out. Then we sent for our mother. Father had died when I was 10. After three years in New York I married."

This is the almost childlike account of the facts of Bubbe's early life. It reminds me of a witness statement, still scarred with trauma, devoid of emotion. These could be the facts of any young immigrant's life, but they don't hint at what was so special about Bubbe. Her irrepressible, infectious joy was our lifeblood—and it stood in stark contrast to Big Bubbe's way of being.

No one in the family has shared a compelling story about what might have caused my bubbling, hugging, nurturing grandmother to choose Big Bubbe at a Jewish community dance, but all the Brenners are glad she did. As Dad wrote it:

"My Mom, Sadie, was the love of my life. She was the symbol of love and tenderness, and she steered me on a road to decent behavior—when some of my community of friends were going in the direction of crime and evil. To have my mother disappointed in me was a fear, but it was embedded in love.

"She was not a very outspoken person, but when put in a corner, would defend herself, as well as her children. She was in a constant battle with my father regarding our upbringing, and she almost always defended us from correction by the belt. After I married your mother and had children, and after Dad died, I would visit her on my day off, Monday. We would have a piece of

Bubbe and her beloved father in Ukraine, circa 1908.

toast and coffee. It made me so happy to see that you children and your mother loved her as much as I. When your grandmother died, it left an empty space in my heart. A desire to hug her, one more time, still lingers."

Sitting in the family station wagon at the cemetery after her burial, I saw my dad weep with abandon for the first and only time. I saw his heart break.

My own memories of Bubbe are imbued with the delicious kitchen aroma of goulash and the sound of her heavily accented voice. She let me trot behind her in the kitchen, holding onto the edge of her apron as if it were a security blanket. I can still conjure sensory snapshots of her, and the environment we inhabited together—her round yet sturdy softness, the tang of the apples from the tree in her yard, the thick bristles along the back of her Basset Hound, Chauncy.

Bubbe's face impossibly showed both the weight of her experience and the irrepressible joy that comes from hope. That's why I always found her to be the personification of the American dream, the person who found opportunity where others saw roadblocks. She poured goodness over every dispute, on every splinter. Milk and honey in a threadbare apron.

"Mom and Pop had their first child (Willie) in New York," my Uncle Freddie told me. "They stayed until there was a bad flu epidemic, and many babies died. The doctor told Sadie to fatten him up to resist illness, and it worked." The small family

Max's sisters—from left, Edna, Florence, and Rose—holding baby Fred, circa 1936.

then moved to Norfolk, Virginia, where Louis—as his brothers, Abe and Harry had done before him—would work in their Uncle Joe's bakery. Uncle Joe helped all of them to perfect the Brenners' signature bread—handmade and delivered by horse and carriage at wholesale prices to retail establishments, including restaurants and grocery stores. In one family configuration or other, the younger Brenners helped Uncle Joe to sell baked goods in Norfolk, Portsmouth, and Newport News—until they would disperse to open their own bakeries. Abe was long gone before Louis ever got there, because of a particular day in 1903 that became family lore. If potential relatives know this story, then I know they are related to me. Here's how Dad told it:

"Abe was in charge of finding the delivery horses. He bought one—I think it was a race horse from the track—and he trained it. When he thought it was ready, he hitched it to the bread wagon. I think the horse did fine for a few days. But one day, with a full load of bread heading to a delivery, the horse was spooked by something and ran off with the whole kit and caboodle. Eventually, the wagon turned over, killing the horse and ruining all the bread. Great-uncle Joe was furious at Abe. Abe didn't think it was his fault, so he quit, then and there. At the train station, even without speaking English well, he made the ticket-seller understand that he wanted to go as far away from Norfolk as possible. Abe ended up in Seattle, Washington. He soon married and opened his own bakery, where he stayed in business for at

least fifty years. There is still a Brenner's Bakery in, ironically, Bellevue, Washington."

When the other boys eventually went their own ways, Harry settled in Baltimore, establishing a bakery that lasted about twenty years. My grandparents moved several times, with Big Bubbe opening a series of bakeries and working at different jobs during the run-up and span of the Great Depression.

Sadie and Louis—Bubbe and Big Bubbe—did not share with their children or grandchildren the folk culture they surely possessed, not even their first languages or religious customs. They simply wanted to be American. They looked at America as a place where their family would not experience the hate and persecution they had endured in Europe. I suspect that my grandparents didn't tell us stories of the Old Country because there were few happy ones. It seems they left that part of life

My grandparents in their kitchen in Washington, DC., circa 1940s.

behind them—along with their Jewishness. They wanted their children to be American, to speak English, to blend, and I know that this message was delivered. Loud and clear.

If anything about our ancestral heritage was mentioned in our family, then Max shut it down. He had been trained to push history aside, and almost never talked about religion. As far as we knew, he was an atheist and the rest of us were secular Americans who went to church on Easter and Christmas Eve. Mostly, we were just American bakers. A whole family of them.

During my dad's childhood, this culture really came to life in the Washington, DC, location, where the family lived upstairs from the bakery—and everyone worked downstairs, at some point or other. In those days, Bubbe was the bakery's only sales person. "She did a great job," he said. "Mom remembered the names of most of the customers, and they loved her. A lot of the customers had credit with her, and most of them were very trustworthy and paid their balances, a little bit, from time to time. Eventually, when they each turned about ten years old, my sisters Florence and Rose helped with sales." Like his brothers, Max began working as soon as he was tall enough to help.

Decades later, he could describe the bakery to me, as if it were yesterday. To the left of the register, there was a section of cases that held rolls and fresh-baked loaves—all uncut. White and wheat, oatmeal, rye, and pumpernickel, French and Italian loaves, cheese bread, and huge round loaves of pumpernickel-and-rye

swirl with cornmeal on the bottom. Some of the rolls were crusty outside and soft inside, like the Kaiser rolls and salt sticks that were braided and topped with chunky salt. Some of the standard hot dog and hamburger rolls had sesame seeds, but Dad described poppy seed and clover leaf rolls—along with whole trays of Parker House rolls that the bakers pulled apart to bag into neat dozens. Each group of six stuck together; two sections were stacked and slid into a plastic bag. I could imagine the delicate dough, folded and golden, a dusting of flour underneath.

Next to a swivel door that led to the back was a black rotary-dial telephone. And the bread cutter—the same one that would cut bread at our bakery decades later. I remember when Dad first allowed me to place a loaf of bread into its V of metal fingers, then pull the thick metal handle that closed the fingers around the loaf. It worked like the handle on a La-Z-Boy chair, except it also triggered the action of serrated blades that sawed back and forth, up through the bread. The violent sawing of the blades vibrated the table and made a great humming, grinding sound. When it was done, the fingers opened with a thud and a clang. I'd slip a plastic bag around the perfectly sliced loaf, and tie it off with a paper-covered wire twist.

The Washington, DC, Brenner's Bakery was primarily a wholesale bread shop. Big Bubbe proofed the dough through the night, and then he baked first thing in the morning. As his sons grew up, they added a few retail sweets to the roster, and one of the products they made was called "Washington Pie." Dad couldn't remember who named it, but it was anything but a pie. "It was made from left-over or stale product, such as bread of any kind—white, rye, pumpernickel—and sweet stuff, like cinnamon buns." First, the bread and sweets were soaked in water overnight in a big bucket. Next day, this mixture was blended with sugar, salt, shortening, and flour, and emptied onto a 16" x 26" sheet pan with a two-inch metal frame inserted along the edges.

"We baked Washington Pie after all other work was finished—the last thing we did was to turn off the oven and leave it in overnight. In the morning, we iced and cut it into twenty-four slices, each weighing about one pound. We sold them for five cents each. Believe it or not, it tasted very good and sold very well. One piece would fill your tummy for the whole day."

In 1953, something inspired Dad's elder brothers to launch another sweet venture. I have only a vague recollection of the "Bren Bear" and "Bren Rabbit" cakes in public, but they were our go-to birthday cakes when we girls were very young. The cakes themselves could be either yellow or chocolate, but the decorations were unique. On one hand, these cartoon-like shapes were meant as a branding tool for the family name; on another hand, the concept celebrated a post-war attitude of fresh thinking and fun possibilities.

In practice, the cakes were sold in the bakery, but they didn't become the marketing hook that the brothers imagined. I've

discovered some archival news stories and photos—as well as the pattern for the patented pans—but nothing indicates that this effort took off in the retail market.

In a tipping of the hat to creativity, however, detailed retro decorating instructions are available on this book's website. In practice, I imagine today's bakers would—and are invited to!—create a very different design, but Brenner's fans might enjoy seeing what the brothers thought was cool, back in the day.

Right: The Brenner brothers, Eddie (far left) and Hymie (far right), offering their newly patented cake pans at a trade show in the 1950s. **Opposite page:** Newspaper photo of my cousin Eddie in an ad about the new product.

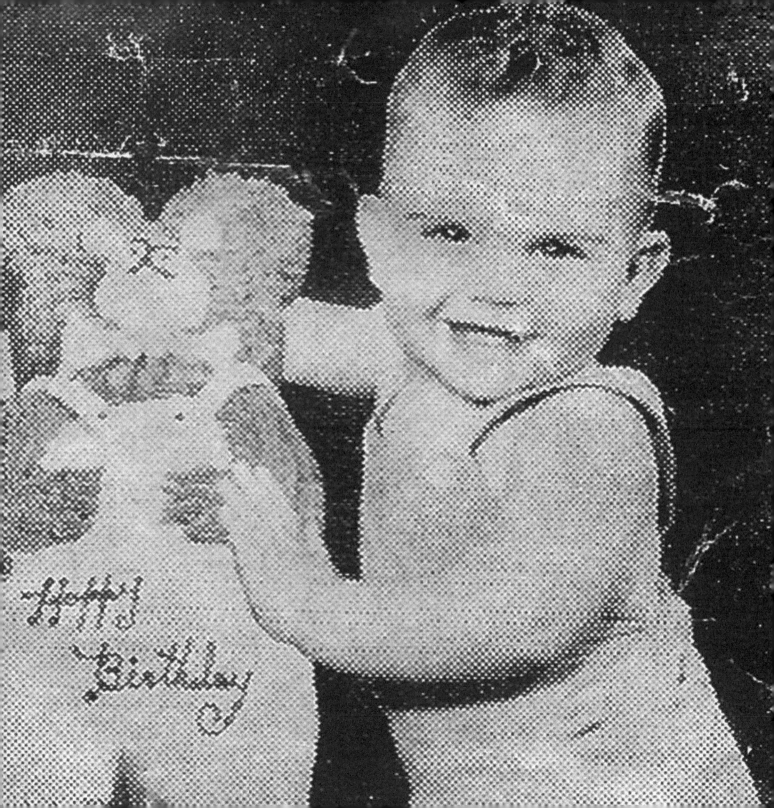

PUTTING 2 AND 2 TOGETHER

As I filtered through these stories—and translated them to my home-kitchen experience—I felt a sense of freedom. My exploration into these recipes, and into my family's past, wasn't coming from a sense of survival. My bottom line, at first anyway, was about the legacy. The more baking I did, the better the food became, and the better I felt I could represent Brenner's.

I developed a baking ritual, in which I deliberately invoked my dad's presence—and my grandfather's. I asked for their help, and they showed up every time. Sometimes I felt the heat of their hands on mine as the yeast slowly sifted through my fingers. I'd already started wearing Dad's aprons, so I added some of his T-shirts to my baking uniform—especially my favorite, depicting the Pillsbury doughboy. I used his baking pans, and saw his handwriting with every recipe.

The bread starting coming out perfectly. The Parker House rolls were heaven. Everything began working so much faster and easier. And I heard Dad's honey voice in my head saying, "That's right baby, just keep baking!"

Maybe all of that is really kind of "expected." Of course I would get better at baking; of course the breads and goodies would come out more consistently. But the real accomplishment was something I wasn't expecting. The more baking I did, the closer I got to my dad. And this book changed, too. As I stepped into my dad's shoes, and his dad's shoes, the project grew from a traditional cookbook into a family history. The moment of truth started with one innocent question: Why milk powder?

It began as just another side road. Like the oleo and shortening conundrum, or experimenting with butter in cookies, I began by wondering why milk powder appeared in several Brenner's bread and cookie recipes. After conducting a little research project, I concluded that there seem to be very practical reasons to use powdered milk, especially in bread dough. For example, in breads, the liquid-to-dry ratios are so important, and eliminating the extra liquid in milk eliminates a variable. Milk powder also adds flavor, and helps with browning, or so the Internet told me.

But this little detour touched a nerve. I'd initially assumed that the bakery didn't use butter and milk because they were too expensive. My second guess had considered the longevity of the baked end-product. Finally, I started wondering about other reasons that people generally avoid animal products, or at least minimize or segregate their use. Keeping in mind that I was reconstituting recipes originating in Europe long before World War I, maybe it should have been obvious from the start.

I turned to my Uncle Freddie, who reminded me of how devout Big Bubbe had been, and that my grandparents had kept a kosher kitchen. I remembered that Yiddish had been their "secret language" at home throughout my childhood—and that they also spoke Hebrew, German, Polish, and Hungarian. I knew that the

bakery in Seattle was referred to as a Jewish or kosher bakery, and that those terms were not used with our bakery. Ever. My dad's bakery didn't make challah bread or other traditionally Jewish items. Until the milk powder exercise, I had been thinking about ingredients. Not religion.

Uncle Freddie described his father as a being deeply Jewish, knowing all of the prayers and rituals—but only going to synagogue rarely, or on high holidays. "His large family was Hassidic," he explained. "They gathered in big rooms to pray, and they had a person leading who was like a rabbi."

The last piece of the puzzle—about our bakery, about our recipes—came from one of the *Brenner's Bakery Memories* Facebook community. The message seemed simple enough, but I was completely unprepared for its implications.

> *We loved your bakery because—back then, from 1968 on—so many cakes were made with lard. Your dad made our cakes with so much love, which gave my kosher/halal family peace of mind when enjoying any treat. It meant so much to us. We couldn't eat cakes from (anywhere else). We would buy them from Brenner's. Every birthday, anniversary, or cupcake was from Brenner's only. My mom lived for your éclairs for afternoon tea. My sister's wedding cake, my wedding cake. Each guest left with a small box of chocolate tops. (Your dad) taught my mom that the green and yellow frosting was not bitter, so all of our cakes were yellow flowers with green leaves and trim.*

These notes and conversations led me into a full-on genealogy project. And that project did more than connect some dots in family history; it spoke to my heart. I discovered where I belong.

As it turns out, my grandfather kept a kosher bakery, and—from what I can tell—so did my dad. The subject had never come up when I worked there, and neither my sisters nor Christine can remember anyone ever asking or talking about it. It's as if the subject that had defined my family's life—but was never discussed—became an undercurrent that held us all up. It fed us, nurtured us, and spread through the community.

Technically, all of Louis and Sadie's children are Jewish, but they didn't celebrate any of the Jewish holidays as a family. Some of Dad's siblings brought chocolate gold-wrapped "coins" at Christmas; that was my first indication that something was different between my extended family and everyone else I knew. Max had married a Gentile at city hall, and neither of their fathers attended the wedding. They said it was because my parents were so young. But whatever it was, by the time we kids were born, Big Bubbe no longer cared if his daughter-in-law was Jewish. He no longer cared if my sisters and I were. Technically.

What he cared about was that we existed. All of us. Any of us. And because his uncle Joe had survived, and Bubbe had survived, and his brothers had survived, these recipes have survived. I hope you love them as much as I do. I hope they make new memories for your families.

WHITE BREAD

The first bread recipe I tried was white bread—because it was Dad's favorite. His typical snack at home was one piece of white bread, maybe with some butter, folded over. More specifically, Dad loved warm white bread. He came home early on Sundays, and always brought home a big box of doughnuts. I'd run out to meet him as he drove into the driveway. Every time, I'd find this lone bag of sliced white bread on the passenger seat. More specifically, I'd find half a loaf. If it was in a plastic bag, there would still be steam and moisture inside.

"You ate our bread on the way home!" I'd tease him. He'd chuckle and tell me not to worry. He always had another loaf for the rest of us.

Makes two one-pound loaves
1 T active dry yeast
4½ c bread flour
⅓ c milk powder
¼ c granulated sugar
1 T salt
2 c water (105–110°F)
⅛ c (2 T) shortening

Prepare proof bowl and proof spot. (For details on how, see Bread Notes, page 269.)

In a standing mixer (or by hand), whisk together yeast, flour, milk powder, sugar, and salt.

Combine water and shortening until mostly melted. Slowly bring this mixture to 105–110°F, either in the microwave or on stovetop.

When I tried making this bread for the first time, I started by warming the yeast in my fingers. I remembered that Dad had said that this recipe—of all of them—was the essence of my grandfather. His philosophy, his spiritual practice. I could almost hear Big Bubbe's voice, whispering to listen to the dough with my hands. When I pulled those first loaves out of the oven, it was as if he had just walked into my kitchen. I ate half the loaf standing at the cutting board.

Mix on setting 1 in the standing mixer with dough hook, slowly adding the warm liquid mixture. Using setting 2, knead for a total of 3–5 minutes (or about 7 minutes by hand) until smooth and silky. The dough will pull away from the dough hook when lifted.

Gently scrape into the prepared bowl. Turn the dough over so the top is oiled. This keeps the dough moist so it won't crack, and rising will be smooth.

Cover with floured plastic and place in the proofing spot (70–90°F) until it almost doubles in size, from 30–90 minutes.

Gently turn the dough out onto a lightly floured surface. Lightly flour hands and top of dough. Cut in half.

For each half, fold and shape for a loaf pan. Place in proof spot, covered with floured plastic, for the final rise. You'll know when it's ready by using the "dimple test." (For details on shaping, see Bread Notes, page 272; for the Dimple Test, page 271.) Preheat oven to 350°F.

Gently brush tops with Egg Wash (page 276).

Bake for 25 minutes at 350°F until very brown on top. Bread will sound hollow when gently tapped. Be patient here; if you want a good crust, don't rush baking. For a softer bread, then bake to a golden brown on top. If the top goes to a deeper brown, then the sides will be just the right amount of crunchy.

Place in a cool spot until cool enough to lift or tilt out of the pan and onto a cooling rack, without collapsing or being mushed in. Please note: If you leave it in the pan until fully cool, it will sweat and the crust will become soft. Take it out too soon, and it will collapse in on itself.

BREAD AND WATER

VARIATION: RAISIN BREAD

Raisin Bread requires only a few deviations from the White Bread recipe, shown on previous pages.

In the mixing process, the only change comes when whisking together the dry ingredients—yeast, flour, milk powder, sugar, and salt. Add the raisins to this mixture.

The next change occurs after the first rise—after the dough has been turned out onto the lightly floured surface and cut in half.

Instead of folding and placing in the pan, roll each section of dough to about ½–1" thick (it will be about 8" x 16" in size). Then, sprinkle each section with half the cinnamon (1T), and loosely roll into a "log." It makes sense to roll from the 8" edge, so that the resulting log is about the same length as a loaf pan. Before placing the log in the pan, tuck in the ends—and *voilà*.

After the final rise, do not brush with Egg Wash (as in White Bread), as these loaves are finished differently:

After baking and cooling completely, drizzle heavily with Powdered Sugar Icing.

In addition to White Bread ingredients:
1 c raisins
2 T cinnamon

Powdered Sugar Drizzle/Icing

6+ c powdered sugar (measure then sift)
⅓+ c milk or water (a little at a time)
⅛ c (2 T) vanilla extract

Mix ingredients. To achieve a pourable consistency, you might need a bit more liquid; add slowly until it's perfect.

BREAD AND WATER

RYE BREAD

Rye bread is my favorite. Especially Pumpernickel. I love all of the rye varieties when toasted, with lots of salted butter. I love everything about the experience—crunchy crust, tart rye twang, the moisture of the sour dough, the caraway (but not too much), the corn meal, how it slices so nicely. Even my loaves that didn't rise were great biscotti.

This is a bread that I identify with my grandfather's Old-World beginnings. It's the most Jewish. Every loaf is different, magnificent, a universe of flavor, texture, memory. It satisfies my folk soul.

Makes two, one-pound loaves or about 24 rolls
2½ t active dry yeast
2 t salt
2 c first clear flour (see note)
2 c bread flour
1½ T whole caraway seeds (optional)
1⅔ c rye sour (page 280)
1⅓ (+ ⅓) c water (105–110°F)

Prepare proof bowl and proof spot. (For details on how, see Bread Notes, page 269.)

Lightly oil the dough hook. Using the mixing bowl with dough hook (or by hand), whisk together yeast, salt, flours, and caraway.

While mixing on low (or gently kneading by hand), add rye sour and then drizzle in water. This is a quick process, only about 1–3 minutes—add tablespoons of water at a time, just until the ingredients are well combined and no longer stringy. Dough should be sticky; you'll have to scrape it off the hook.

Let rest in bowl, covered with floured plastic, for 15 minutes.

Gently scrape out onto a lightly floured board or surface, using a spatula, if needed. Resist adding flour to the mixture, but apply flour to your hands. Fold dough by bringing the top over to the bottom and gently pressing the seam together with the heal of your hand. Then turn the dough a quarter turn and do same for each of the four sides. You can gently pat the dough if there are air bubbles. Gently shape into a ball.

Set in your proof spot to rise. Allow dough to rise until puffy but not quite doubled in size, about 30–40 minutes. You should check your rising dough every 10 minutes, so it won't over-proof.

Gently turn the dough out onto a lightly floured surface. Lightly flour hands and top of dough. Cut in half. For each half, fold and shape for a baking sheet, pan or rolls. (For shapes, see Bread Notes, page 272.)

Cover loosely with floured plastic and set in your proof spot to rise. This rise should be quick, no more than about 10 minutes. Check every few minutes with the Dimple Test (page 271). Before the end of the final rise, preheat oven to 350°F.

Gently brush top with Egg Wash (page 276) or spritz with water. And, if you'd like to score your bread, now is the time. (See how in Bread Notes, page 275.) It's also time to sprinkle with caraway seeds, sesame seeds, bagel "everything" seed combo…whatever toppings you like. Place into the oven.

Bake about 50–55 minutes, until deep golden brown. Bread will sounds hollow when gently tapped, and feels "lighter." Internal temperature should be about 200°F, if you use a digital bread thermometer. For a nice crust, don't under bake. Finally, let it cool completely before slicing to avoid compressing the loaf.

Variation—Pumpernickel Bread: Remove the caraway seeds and add 4 T unsweetened cocoa powder (for color). Everything else is the same!

Note—First Clear Flour: First clear flour balances the texture and rise of rye bread; I order it from King Arthur Flour www.kingarthurflour.com.

BREAD AND WATER

PUMPERNICKEL/ RYE MARBLE LOAF

There are three challenges with this recipe.

The first is to make enough Rye Sour (see page 280). You'll need at least a 50-ounce jar to make the 3⅓ cups of Rye Sour that this recipe calls for—which takes a few extra days of care and feeding. I figure that if you're going to make a batch of the best bread you've ever made at home, it might as well be two loaves. However, you can halve both recipes and just make one if you like.

The second challenge is space. The ultimate final rising spot for both loaves is the single baking sheet they'll both be baked on. In my kitchen, the only proof spot that is big enough for that is the oven. It's important for the proper rise to not let the loaves touch—not at any point in the process—so space the two balls of dough as far into the corners of the baking sheet as you can, without spilling over the edge (4" between loaves and from pan edges). If it looks like they will touch, then slip a strip of parchment between them before they do.

The last consideration is timing. I premeasure and prepare all ingredients for both recipes so that after I mix up one, I can set it aside in a separate bowl for first proof while I make the other one. Then the proof time is only a few minutes different. You can always put dough in the refrigerator (or outside if it's cold) to slow it down if needed.

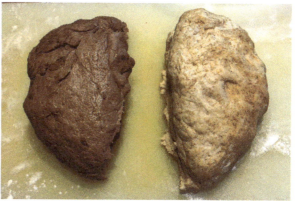

Follow the Rye Bread and Pumpernickel Bread recipes (Page 42) until the first rise has completed. Then:

Gently turn dough out onto a floured work surface, chop in half and chop each half into six pieces, for both recipes. You will have 12 pieces of Rye and 12 pieces of Pumpernickel. Make a pile of 6 pieces of Rye and 6 pieces of Pumpernickel and gently knead them together until combined into a smooth, well-formed ball. About 3 minutes. Then roll the dough under lightly floured, open hands against the lightly floured surface (which provides some friction) to form a smooth ball. Use the "bread fairy" Danielle's stretching method (Bread Notes page 274) to finish the 2# round boule loaf.

Place the dough into a parchment-lined bowl that has been sprinkled lightly with medium corn meal (if desired) for the final rise—using the Dimple Test (page 271) to confirm that it's done. Do the same with the other 12 pieces of Rye and Pumpernickel.

Makes 2, two-pound round "boule" loaves

BREAD AND WATER

This recipe embodies the bakery for me, as I think it did for Big Bubbe. Pumpernickel/Rye Marble Bread is the pinnacle of our family story; it's also symbolic of the Melting Pot. Everything comes together here.

Before the end of the final rise, preheat oven to 350°F. When final proof is complete, use the parchment to gently lift each loaf out of the proof bowl and onto a baking sheet. Space them as described above, so that they don't touch one another or spill over the pan's edge. Fold and tuck the parchment as needed.

At this point you can Egg Wash or spritz, score/slash, and top the loaves as desired per the above recipes.

Bake as indicated, except these large loaves take longer to bake, about 60–70 min. Be sure to bake long enough for a nice, deep, golden crust, a hollow sound, and a light feel when it's done. Internal temperature should be about 200°F.

BREAD AND WATER

PARKER HOUSE DINNER ROLLS

Makes about 4 dozen rolls
1½ T active dry yeast
5 c bread flour
⅓ c milk power
1 T salt
¾ c granulated sugar
2 c lukewarm water (105–110°F)
¾ c shortening
2 eggs, lightly beaten

STAGE 1 PREPARATION

Prepare a half-sheet baking sheet, preferably with 1" sides, with parchment.

Prepare proof bowl and proof spot. (For details on how, see Bread Notes, page 269.)

Whisk together yeast, flour, milk powder, salt, and sugar in medium mixing bowl or standing mixer bowl with bread hook attachment.

Combine water and shortening until mostly melted; add eggs. Bring this mixture slowly to 105–110°F, either in the microwave or on stovetop.

Using a standing mixer or by hand, slowly drizzle in the liquid mixture, scraping the side of the bowl and dough hook/spoon. Mix for a minute or so on speed 1 to combine, scrape side of

bowl. Turn dough over, and then knead on speed 2 for a minute or so, just until dough is combined and smooth. Don't overwork. If kneading by hand, about 3 minutes. Gravity will pull the dough away from the beater/spoon when lifted; the dough will not stick to the sides of the bowl.

Scrape dough into the proof bowl and flip so the top is oiled, too. Set dough aside in your warm proof spot, covered with floured plastic for about 2 hours, until almost doubled in size.

STAGE 2 PREPARATION – TRADITIONAL PARKER ROLLS
Gently turn the dough out onto a lightly floured surface. Lightly flour hands and top of dough.

Separate dough into 3 or 4 sections. You'll work with just one at a time, so roll all but the first section into balls under your open hands, and cover with floured plastic to rest until their turns.

For each section: Roll out to a ½"–thick rectangle, about 8" x 16". Gently pat to remove air bubbles, then cut in half lengthwise (each half 4" x 16"). Roll out each half, again to ½" thick. (If desired, generously paint or drizzle melted butter down the middle of the long narrow rectangle.) Fold dough lengthwise almost in half—leaving a slight edge showing, perhaps ½ inch. With rolling pin or the heel of your hand, press down along the seam, sealing the dough to that edge. With chopping knife, pizza cutter, or scraper, cut into 6 or 7 equal-sized rolls. Do the same with the other piece. You might make yours larger or smaller, but Brenner's were about 2" x 2" raw, 3½" x 3½" finished.

Place cut rolls ¼" away from one another and ½" from the edge of baking sheet. (This spacing will allow them room to rise again and eventually touch.)

PROOFING & BAKING
Set pans in your warm proof place to rise, covered with floured plastic. Let rise to almost doubled in size, about 30–90 minutes. Use the Dimple Test (page 271) to determine when they're done. Before the end of the final rise, preheat oven to 350°F.

Gently brush with Egg Wash (page 276) for a glossy finish like Brenner's. You can gently brush with melted butter for a browned, matte finish.

Bake at 350°F until deep golden brown, about 25–30 minutes. Don't under bake.

VARIATIONS – ALTERNATE SHAPES
Although Parker House rolls are known for their signature shape, there's nothing that says you can't make them your own way.

Round Dinner rolls
First, shape each piece of dough into a rough ball by pulling the dough together at the bottom. Then, roll it around under the palm of your hand and fingers into a smooth ball. This works best if your surface has a bit of friction that smooths the dough, and lightly flouring the surface does the trick. Pinch dough together underneath to make a tight ball, and set on baking sheet to rise. Place rolls 2" inches apart. Then proof and bake.

Clover Leaf rolls
Divide each of the roll pieces into three very small pieces. Roll each piece into a little ball, tucking the dough under for a smooth, round ball, then place all three balls together into same cup of a greased or lined muffin tin. Then proof and bake.

Round Twists Rolls
Roll out each of the pieces into a log, then make an "O," but don't join the ends. Instead, tuck one end up through the O, as if you're starting to tie a knot. Proof and bake.

If desired, you can brush with butter when the rolls are right out of the oven, for an extra buttery flavor.

BREAD AND WATER

BAGELS

The bakers made bagels first thing on Tuesdays, the first day back after being closed Mondays. While they were at it, my dad made mini-bagel "teething rings" for his grandchildren. He put them into the freezer and hauled them out for teething babies. These mini-bagels were easy to hold, unlikely to cause anyone to choke, and were yummy.

    Until this book, I'd never made bagels before, and I knew they required a little finesse. I was worried I wouldn't get them right. However, when I first heard the "thwap" of the bagel dough—as it was kneading in my standing mixer—I just smiled. I didn't even know I knew that sound, but I remembered it. And after they were all done, I smelled the warm, steamy, doughy, oily water simmering on the stove. That smell flooded back as one of the distinct components of the bakery.

STAGE 1 PREPARATION

Prepare proof bowl and proofing spot. (For details on how, see Bread Notes, page 269.)

In a standing mixer or mixing bowl, combine yeast, flour, sugar, and salt. Whisk together.

Combine warm water and oil. Bring this mixture gently to 105–110°F in microwave or on stovetop.

With dough hook attachment on a standing electric mixer (or by hand), slowly stir in the warm liquid mixture, scraping the side of the bowl and dough hook/spoon. Mix for a minute on speed 1 to combine, and then knead on speed 2 for 3–5 minutes until dough is smooth and silky. If kneading by hand, about 7–10 minutes. If using a standing mixer, you will begin to hear the classic "thwap" sound of bagel dough as it kneads. The dough will be smooth and will come away from the beater/spoon when ready. Resist the temptation to add flour.

Scrape dough into the prepared bowl. Set dough aside in your proof spot, covered with floured plastic about 1–2 hours, until almost but not doubled in size.

Makes about 24 small bagels
4 t active dry yeast
4½ c bread flour
¼ c granulated sugar
4 t salt
2 c water
⅛ c vegetable oil
½ large pot of water (about 2 quarts)
⅛ c brown sugar
1 T granulated sugar

BREAD AND WATER

STAGE 2 PREPARATION & PROOFING

Start a pot of water on the stove, add sugars, stir and bring to a gentle boil.

Gently turn the dough out onto a lightly floured surface. Lightly flour hands and top of dough. Cut in half. For each half, fold and let each half of dough rest under floured plastic.

Cut dough into 24 pieces (½ in each half) for small bagels (Brenner's Bakery size), larger pieces for larger bagels. I eyeball them, but you can weigh them if uniform size is desired.

Working with one piece at a time, roll out to a log the size of a sausage, about 6+ inches long, and join the ends, tucking dough under with a light press or pinch. Place each on a baking sheet lined with greased parchment, and then place full baking sheet(s) into the proofing spot, covered with floured plastic, to rise for about 15 minutes. They'll puff up a little. If you want more time before cooking, then you can refrigerate them at this point—just let them puff back up for 30 minutes or so before boiling.

BOILING & BAKING
Preheat oven to 400°F.

Bring water to boil, then back it off to a hot simmer before dropping in the dough.

Place as many shaped pieces of dough as will fit without crowding into the simmering water. I can fit 3–4 small ones in my big soup pot. Allow to float for 1–2 minutes and turn over. Let float for 1–2 minutes then transfer to a parchment-lined baking pan.

At this point you can brush with an Egg Wash (see page 276) and bake plain, or top with sesame seeds, poppy seeds, "everything" mixture or anything you like before baking.

Bake for about 23–27 minutes until deep golden brown.

Variations:
Add any one of a variety of ingredients—in the last minute of the first kneading. Try raisins, cinnamon, blueberries, cheese, olives, onions, sundried tomatoes, or garlic, and then proceed as instructed.

BREAD AND WATER

EGG BREAD

**Makes two,
one-pound loaves**

¼ c active dry yeast
5¼ c bread flour
⅓ c granulated sugar
1 T salt
2 c warm water
⅓ c vegetable oil
2 eggs

Lightly grease two loaf pans.

Prepare proof bowl and proof spot. (For details on how, see Bread Notes, page 269.)

In a standing mixer (or by hand) combine yeast, flour, sugar, and salt.

Add oil and eggs to water and bring to 105–110°F. When warming, do so gradually in a microwave oven or on the stovetop.

Mix on setting 1 in standing mixer with a dough hook, slowly adding the warm liquid mixture. Using setting 2, knead for 3–5 minutes (about 7 minutes by hand) until smooth and silky.

Gently turn out and scrape into the prepared bowl. Turn the dough over so the top is oiled, or oil the top if the dough is too sticky to turn over. This keeps it moist so dough won't crack and rising will be smooth.

Cover with floured plastic and place in your warm proofing spot (70–90°F) until almost doubled in size.

Gently turn the dough out onto a lightly floured surface. Lightly flour hands and top of dough. Cut dough in half. For each half, fold and shape for a loaf pan. (For techniques, see Bread Notes, page 272.)

Place in proof spot, covered with floured plastic, for the final rise. This dough is lively; only 15 minutes might do it, so watch closely—and use the Dimple Test (page 271) to confirm when it's done.

Before the end of the final rise, preheat oven to 350°F.

Gently brush tops with Egg Wash (page 276.)

Bake for 20–25 minutes until very brown on top. Bread will sound hollow when gently tapped. Be patient here—if you want a good crust, don't rush baking. If the top is deep brown, the sides will be just the right amount of crunchy.

BREAD AND WATER

FRENCH BREAD

Prepare proof bowl and proof spot. (For details on how, see Bread Notes, page 269.)

In a standing mixer bowl or by hand, combine yeast, flour, sugar, and salt. In another bowl or saucepan, combine warm water, oil, and egg. Bring the warm liquid mixture gently to 105–110°F, in microwave or on stovetop.

With a dough hook attachment (or by hand), slowly stir in the warm liquid mixture, scraping the side of the bowl and dough hook/spoon. Mix for 1 minute on speed 1 to combine and then knead on speed 2 for 3–5 minutes until dough is smooth and silky. If kneading by hand, about 7 minutes. When dough is ready, it will pull away from the beater/spoon when lifted, but the dough won't come away from the sides of the bowl. It will appear more like strands. The dough will be very sticky, so resist the temptation to add flour, after the first rise it will be much more manageable.

Scrape dough into the prepared bowl. Set dough aside in proof spot, covered with floured plastic, for about 1–2 hours, until almost doubled in size.

Gently turn the dough out onto a lightly floured surface. Lightly flour hands and top of dough. This procedure is for baguettes, but process is similar for all shapes. Cut into four equal pieces. Shape into baguettes. Fold a bath towel in half, and place on baking sheet; then form two "troughs" and then cover towel with parchment. Place baguettes, two per baking sheet, in the troughs.

Makes 2 football-shaped "bâtard" loaves, 2 round "boule" loaves or 4 long, skinny "baguette" loaves. For details on forming all of these shapes, see Bread Notes, page 272.

1½ t active dry yeast
4 ⅔ c bread flour
⅛ c granulated sugar
1 T salt
⅛ c vegetable oil
1 egg, lightly beaten
2 c warm water (105–110°F)

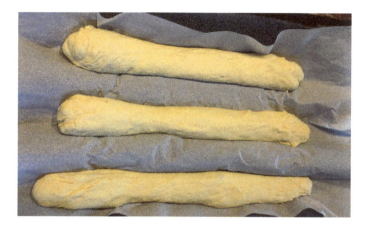

Set trays in your proof spot to rise. Allow dough to rise until puffy but not quite doubled in size, about 30–40 minutes. Check your rising dough every 10 minutes so it won't over-proof; use the Dimple Test (page 271) to confirm when it's done.

Before the end of the final rise, preheat oven to 350°F.

After the rise is complete, gently remove towel (leaving parchment on baking sheet). Then, you may score the top of your bread (see Bread Notes on Scoring Bread, page 275).

Use Egg Wash or spritz with water, and then top your bread, too, if preferred. For details and topping ideas, see Topping Bread in Bread Notes (page 276).

Place baguettes into the oven while preheating to achieve a nice extra rise, and bake for 35 minutes at 350°F until deep brown. Loaves will sound hollow when gently tapped and will feel lighter. Be patient; if you want a good crust, don't rush baking.

SOUR FRENCH BREAD

**Makes 2 football-shaped "bâtard" loaves.
For details on forming the shape, see Bread Notes, page 272.**
1 T active dry yeast
4 c bread flour
⅓ c milk powder
1 T salt
½ c sourdough starter (page 278)
2 c warm water (105–110°F)

Prepare proof bowl and proof spot. (For details on how, see Bread Notes, page 269.)

In a standing mixer bowl or hand-mixing bowl, combine yeast, flour, milk powder, and salt. Once these are blended, add sourdough starter—use more if you want more sour flavor.

In the standing mixer bowl with dough hook (or by hand), slowly add the warm water. Knead for 3–5 minutes (about 7 minutes by hand) or until smooth and dough just starts to pull away from the dough hook when lifted.

Gently turn out dough into the prepared proof bowl. Cover with floured plastic and place in the warm proofing spot (70–90°F) until dough has almost doubled in size.

Gently turn the dough out onto a lightly floured surface. Lightly flour hands and top of dough. Cut in half. For each half, fold and shape into bâtards for a baking sheet.

Place in proof spot, covered with floured plastic, for the final rise. Use the Dimple Test (page 271) to confirm when it's done.

Before the end of the final rise, preheat oven to 350°F.

Gently brush tops with Egg Wash (page 276).

Bake for 25 minutes at 350°F until golden brown. It will sound hollow when gently tapped. Be patient here, if you want a good crust, don't rush baking.

CROISSANTS

**Makes about
2 dozen small rolls**
2 T active dry yeast
3¾ c bread flour
½ c granulated sugar
¼ c milk powder
1 T salt
1 c water (105–110°F)
⅓ c margarine/butter
2 egg whites
(lightly beaten)
Additional 1½ c (3 sticks)
margarine/butter

STAGE 1 PREPARATION

Bring all ingredients to room temperature, except the second portion (3 sticks) of margarine/butter.

Prepare two parchment-lined baking sheets.

Whisk together yeast, flour, sugar, milk powder, and salt in the standing mixer bowl.

Prepare warm water, add ⅓ c margarine/butter and egg whites. Gently bring back up to 105–110°F temperature, in the microwave or on stovetop.

Slowly add warm water mixture to the dry mixture while mixing by hand or on level 1. Scrape sides and hook. If needed, add a few more tablespoons of water to give it enough moisture to come together without making it too sticky.

Mix at level 1 for about 3–5 minutes until dough is smooth and elastic—just past sticky. Don't use a higher setting, as you don't want to incorporate a bunch of air.

Press/pat into a square shape, loosely wrap with floured plastic, and place in the refrigerator for 20–30 minutes.

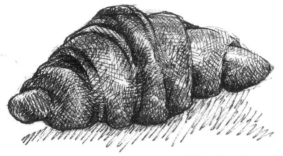

STAGE 2 PREPARATION

Prepare the second measure of margarine/butter (3 sticks): Divide into equal parts, working with a stick and a half at a time. Cut in half lengthwise to make four pieces. Lay them on plastic wrap to make a rectangle. Cover with another piece of plastic wrap. Pound and roll with a rolling pin to form a rectangle about 6" x 9" and put it in the fridge to chill until dough is ready. You'll have two pieces, each formed of 1½ sticks of margarine/butter.

Flour a surface or board very well and place half the dough on the surface (put other half back in refrigerator). Roll with a well-floured rolling pin, forming the dough into a rectangle about 10" x 16". Be sure to keep flour on the surface under the dough, too. Gently pat the air bubbles out as needed.

Place half of one of the chilled margarine/butter pieces in the middle of the rectangle, and fold dough over it, left and right, to make a smaller rectangle package. Rotate one-quarter turn and roll back out to the large rectangle size, place the other half of the margarine/butter, fold left and right to make another dough package. Press/pinch the ends and the folded edge together to seal the package.

Do the same for the other half of the dough and margarine/butter. Place both back in the refrigerator for 30 minutes.

Margarine versus butter: Croissants are known for their buttery taste—but that taste, in general, happens with either butter or margarine. If you have a very discerning palate, then you can choose based on these criteria:
(1) If you want them to be exactly like Brenner's, then use margarine.
(2) I think they're a very tiny tad more delicious with butter. (Don't tell Big Bubbe.) Try them both ways!

A BAKER'S DAUGHTER

FINISHING

For each package/half, repeat and fold as above (but without adding butter!): roll out to 10" x 16", fold twice; roll again and fold twice—four folds in total, per half. Place back in refrigerator for at least 2 hours, but overnight is better.

Take one dough package at a time out of the fridge and roll out to a 12" x 18" rectangle. Make two lengthwise cuts with a pizza cutter or pastry knife (to make three long sections) then make one cut down the middle to make 6 rectangles. Cut each rectangle in half diagonally to make long triangles.

Working with one triangle at a time, roll it out a bit with a rolling pin. This is when you can put about a tablespoon of a filling of your choice, sweet or savory. Then roll the dough with your fingers from the short edge toward the point of the triangle, curving the roll to a crescent shape. Place on parchment-lined baking sheet. Do same for the rest of the triangles.

PROOFING & BAKING

Let rise at room temperature for about 30–90 minutes until puffy—and use the Dimple Test (page 271) to confirm when it's done.

Near the end of the rising time, preheat oven to 425°F.

Just before putting in the oven, brush the tops with Egg Wash (page 276) and bake for 15 minutes. Reduce oven temp to 350°F and bake for about 15 minutes more until deep golden brown—even down into where the dough overlaps, otherwise they will be under baked.

Variations:
For sweet fillings: chocolate (of course!), almond, cinnamon, fruit pie fillings. For savory: meat, cheese, spinach/veg/ham. Use your imagination!

OATMEAL BREAD

**Makes two,
one-pound loaves**
1 T active dry yeast
3 c bread flour
2½ T whole wheat flour
⅓ c old-fashioned rolled oats
1 T milk powder
1½ t salt
2 c water
1½ T shortening
7½ t honey

Prepare proof bowl and proof spot. (For details on how, see Bread Notes, page 269.)

In a standing mixer bowl (or by hand) combine yeast, flours, oats, milk powder, and salt.

Pour hot water into a glass measuring cup, add the shortening and honey to dissolve. Gently bring this mixture to 105–110°F using the microwave or stovetop.

Mix on setting 1 in standing mixer with dough hook, slowly adding the warm liquid mixture. Using setting 2, knead for 3–5 minutes (about 7 minutes by hand) until smooth and silky. The dough will pull away from the dough hook when you lift it, but it might not fully pull from the sides of the bowl.

Gently turn out and scrape into the prepared bowl. Turn the dough over so the top is oiled, or oil the top if the dough is too sticky to turn over. This keeps it moist so dough won't crack and rising will be smooth.

Set in proof spot to rise. Allow dough to rise until puffy, but not quite doubled in size.

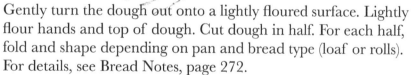

Gently turn the dough out onto a lightly floured surface. Lightly flour hands and top of dough. Cut dough in half. For each half, fold and shape depending on pan and bread type (loaf or rolls). For details, see Bread Notes, page 272.

Place in proof spot, covered with floured plastic, for the final rise, using the Dimple Test (page 271) to confirm when it's done.

Before the end of the final rise, preheat oven to 350°F.

Gently brush tops with Egg Wash (page 276) or spritz with water and sprinkle with oats. Put back in the oven while it is preheating to achieve a nice, extra rise.

Bake for 25–35 minutes at 350°F until very brown on top. Bread will sound hollow when gently tapped and will feel lighter.

WHOLE WHEAT BREAD

**Makes two,
one-pound loaves**

1 T active dry yeast
⅛ c (2 T) milk powder
2 c bread flour
2 c whole wheat flour
1 T salt
1 t unsweetened cocoa powder (for caramel color)
1½ c water (105–110°F)
⅛ c (2 T) shortening
1½ T molasses
1½ T honey
2 eggs, lightly beaten

Prepare proof bowl and proof spot. (For details on how, see Bread Notes, page 269.)

In a standing mixer (or by hand) thoroughly combine yeast, milk powder, bread flour, whole wheat flour, salt, and cocoa.

Combine water and shortening until mostly melted. Add eggs. Bring this mixture slowly to 105–110°F, either in the microwave or on stovetop. Slowly adding the warm liquid mixture, mix until combined on setting 1 in standing mixer with dough hook (or by hand, about a minute or less).

Add molasses and honey. Scrape sides and hook.

Using setting 2, knead for 3–5 minutes (about 7 minutes by hand) until smooth and silky. The dough will pull away from the dough hook when lifted.

Cover the bowl with floured plastic and let sit in your warm proof spot for 20 minutes.

Using setting 2, knead for 7 minutes (about 10 minutes by hand) until smooth and silky. The dough will want to pull away from the dough hook when you lift it, and it just starts to pull away from the sides of the mixing bowl. The dough will be very wet.

Gently turn out and scrape into the prepared bowl. Spray top with cooking oil or turn the dough over in the bowl if it's not too wet to do this. This keeps it moist so it won't crack, and rising will be smooth.

Cover with floured plastic and place in your warm proofing spot (70–90°F) until it almost doubles in size.

Gently turn the dough out onto a lightly floured surface. Lightly flour hands and top of dough. Cut in half. For each half, fold and shape depending on pan and bread type (loaf or rolls). For details, see Bread Notes, page 272.

Place in proof spot, covered with floured plastic, for the final rise. Use the Dimple Test (page 271) to confirm that it's done.

Before the end of the final rise, preheat oven to 350°F.

Bake at 350°F for 20 minutes, then tent bread with foil and bake 20 more. It will be very brown on top. It will sound hollow when gently tapped. Be patient here, if you want a good crust, don't rush baking. For a softer bread, then bake until brown on top. If the top goes to a deeper brown, then the sides will be the perfect amount of crispy.

CHAPTER 3
THE BAKERY

Nowadays, they are called strip malls, those nondescript lines of storefronts, built for convenience. They sprung up before "box stores" were a thing, before anyone but Macy's and Tiffany's spent time on fancy displays. You wouldn't think that magic could happen in a strip mall. But it did. Every day.

If I close my eyes right now, I can feel and see every step to our front door. It is as if Dad's parking space was poured and painted just for him, as if the pavement belonged to our family. I imagine stepping over the cracks, looking for where the curb had a piece nicked out of it. The storefront was brick, with a couple of dozen large square panes of glass flanked by a framed sign. White block letters read B-R-E-N-N-E-R'-S B-A-K-E-R-Y. This would become one of the first things I could spell.

THE CALENDAR

I marked the holidays by the decorations the ladies put in the window. Spray snow in December, eggs and bunnies at Easter, and turkeys in November. Today, as I play back a cherished mental reel of our routines, I realize that these decorations were nothing special; they were the same cardboard and tinsel and crepe paper that small family businesses have strung up for generations. But for me, they flocked every defining moment I witnessed in my childhood. It was because people came to see us during holidays. National holidays, religious holidays, birthdays, weddings, retirements, anniversaries.

Our bakery storefront in Alexandria, Virginia. This is how it looked throughout my childhood. Today, a bakery called Bread & Water Company is housed in this location.

It was understood in our family that as soon as you were old enough, you'd work at the bakery during the holidays, no matter what. I couldn't wait to be old enough. I wanted to go with the adults and work through the night—every night before the eve of a major holiday. Instead, because I was the youngest, at first it was my job to babysit my niece and nephews. For at least a few years, before it was my turn, I watched as my sisters got to go; I watched the door close behind them.

When it was my turn, I devoured every moment. I scrutinized how each family member chipped in, in any way possible. We tested the mettle of a new boyfriend, and even a husband, by how he handled a bakery all-nighter. We would arrive when the bakery closed, two nights before the holiday. For Thanksgiving, we started on Tuesday night; on Christmas, December 23rd. We would work from about 10 p.m. until about 10 a.m., however long it took.

To this day, I think of holidays as orders. Thanksgiving was mostly pies and rolls—hundreds of orders were waiting for us, impaled on a pointed metal skewer attached to a wooden base. We pre-built hundreds of boxes, prepped extra plastic bags, reloaded the wrapping string, and created an assembly line in the front. We organized a separate checkout location, by the decorated cakes, for order pickup only. We numbered all the orders, packed them, stacked them in numeric order, and taped tickets on the outside. We logged the orders in a notebook, also in numerical order, with the customers' names and phone numbers.

Students captured in a Brenner's Bakery ad, printed in the Edison High School yearbook (Alexandria, Virginia), late 1960s. These two, Kim and Steve Messinger, were in the class of 1973, and they've been married for almost 40 years.

The baking schedule gradually sped up through October and November, and each holiday was like the end of a marathon. One after another. The season started in early November, when we would begin to see less of Dad. He reminded me of Santa—shuttled off to the workshop, a servant to the community—disappearing until the crescendo of Christmas Eve.

Then December would arrive. With parties and events, customers were ordering all month. It was not just pies and rolls. It was everything. Every day, all month long. The usual cookies, pies, rolls, cakes, along with specialty miniature rolls and breads, holiday breads, pastries, and holiday cookies. And Christmas itself was another thing altogether. During the holiday week, Dad started at least a day earlier than everyone else. He worked as hard or harder than his crew, but all the bakers worked around the clock. A few times we found Dad napping on the flour sacks down in the basement, grabbing a few winks before the next batch was ready to mix, or while waiting for the oven timer.

What I loved best was the teamwork. Second was the dough. I have always loved raw dough. During one holiday marathon, I was chewing on the last of a few wonderful little balls of raw dough—I'd popped them in my mouth from a tray waiting for the oven. Dad was standing nearby, unloading the hot trays. I heard him say, "Where is the rest of this miniature rye roll order?" He turned and scanned the tray. He looked at me. I looked at him, my puffed-out cheeks and wide eyes betraying me. My heart sank.

But as tired and frustrated as my dad must have been in that moment, all he said was, "Shit!" And he started another batch.

That year, dawn couldn't come fast enough. Like clockwork, the ladies-in-the-front arrived early, as they did on the eve of every holiday. It was an honored changing of the guard. We were sleep deprived, covered in flour and sugar, our fingers cut and sore from boxing up orders with string, our feet and legs screaming, our bellies ready for breakfast. Grateful that all the baking and packing was done, that everyone had gotten what they needed, that we had made it, we tucked Dad into the back of the station wagon. We drove to breakfast, then somehow found the energy to drive home and crawl into bed. Most years, we would wake up in time to start cooking our own holiday meal, or for Christmas Eve festivities. Sometimes we went to a church service or into DC to see the national and state Christmas trees.

By each Christmas Day, Dad and the bakers would have been working straight since their last vacation, the week of July Fourth. The week between Christmas and New Year's Day is still a sacred week in my house. I stay in my pajamas, lock the front door, turn off the phone, and snuggle in. That was always our recovery time, our family time. We ate cookies out of our own white boxes, tied with string by our cramped fingers. Once I was big enough to help, I loved that my fingers would take all week to heal. And later, when I would play concerts, guitar and mandolin strings would cut my fingers. It didn't bother me a bit. It felt like family.

Still to this day, when the holidays approach, I feel like I am supposed to be at the bakery, doing something important, packing orders, driving Dad home. But even without those familiar team sports—and even before this project—I would bake a few holiday goodies. Now I bake a boat-load.

I hear the tinkling of the front bell that hangs from a string off the inside handle. I hear it clang if I'm the one coming through the door—but the sound of that bell jangling against the metal door frame is chaotic enough that it always gets my attention, no matter where I am in the bakery. If it's after hours, there's also that extra sound, the Dad-only sound, of the large stainless-steel key ring. All the extra keys clank as he twists the ring around to unlock and relock the door.

As the heavy glass door opens, my memory shifts. It's no longer about sounds. Instead, I'm surrounded by smells—sweet, savory, spicy—and then my eyes dart along the U-shaped display case. Which cookies are out? How many pastries? Which of my favorites are there enough of?

Customers head left into the center of the storefront display cases, inside the U of deep golden-patinaed wood, brass trim, and glass. They lean down to peer at the trays of baked goods. But I get to go straight ahead, against the wall, behind the cases, where the ladies are. Where the cookie cases are on my left. I drift my hand along the glass, all the way down to the first corner of cases. Sugar, oatmeal chocolate chip, Mexican wedding, fruit bars, peanut butter, and everyone's favorite, Chocolate Top cookies. These cases are tall, reaching from the floor to way over my head. I can't reach the top, maybe not even the middle shelves. The premade little white boxes are stacked neatly on the tippy-top; the first time I'll be allowed to fill and tie them with the white string, I'll be seven or eight years old. I will perfect my technique on Mondays, when the bakery is closed. I'll bring a friend, and we'll "play bakery." We practice and practice, filling white boxes with day-old cookies and breads and rolls, even pies. But I won't graduate to the holiday all-nighter until I'm about fourteen.

On the other side of the bakery, on the other leg of the U, are the cakes. Devil's food, a rich chocolate, or the vanilla cakes, pre-iced with chocolate, vanilla, or a combination of vanilla sides and chocolate tops—or vice versa. Some are layered, some are whole or half sheets. They have piping and scallops and roses with stems and leaves. Customers can have anything written on them, but typically, they choose Happy Birthday, Happy Anniversary, or Happy Graduation. People tend to rely on the bakery to help them; their creativity is exhausted by all the details of their event, and sometimes they look at a scrap of paper from their pockets. They borrow our pencil, and check "bakery" off the list.

On the top glass shelf of the cake case is a little girl's wonderland. All the miniature theme decorations stand at attention there, waiting to be chosen. I am always partial to the

pink plastic ballerinas, some with an indentation for a candle, but there are also little wooden train sets, baseball players, soldiers, horses in various poses, flat plastic clovers, leprechauns, and carousels. I poke through this case often, dreaming of what I'll have on my next birthday cake, when summer finally arrives.

Behind the U, against the wall shared by the kitchen, are more cabinets. Doughnuts and bread loaves, rolls. On either side are the swivel doors that lead to the back. Each can swing in or out and has a round, thick glass window at grown-up eye level. It's a gamble for me every time I walk past one, or decide to push through, because I'm not tall enough to see through the window, and I can't tell if the door is about to burst open. I learn to dodge those doors, sacrificing an elbow or a knee in order to protect brownies and Chocolate Tops from sure disaster.

As delicious as the front of the bakery is, I love the back just as well; it's where everything happens. When I'm successfully invisible, I hear stories that the bakers would never say in front of me. Sometimes I'm successfully invisible in plain sight, maybe near the big, wooden work table. A shelf runs down the middle that holds sugar, cinnamon, and other sprinkly things; it separates the work surface into two sides, and the bakers can reach the sprinkles from either one.

This is also where the dough from the proof box is shaped and made ready to bake. And on the end of the counter is a tray that holds the slabs of cake that are cut off when a baker levels the

Above: The cake case, with its top shelf of magical decorations. **Opposite page:** And then there were cookies. I grew up in heaven.

 layers, readying a cake for decorating. These are a delicacy that we all enjoy.

The bakers are men of different colors, and Dad hires mentally disabled adults, mostly men, to wash dishes and help in the back. They all love the camaraderie of the kitchen. I am the boss's daughter, so they treat me with the greatest of respect and kindness. A deference that feels unnecessary. Still, it's in this setting that I realize this is a man's world, and if I want to be a part of it, I am going to have to be tough. From listening to Dad at home, I know which ones have drinking or drug problems, trouble at home, or a medical condition. I, too, treat them with respect—and I learn so much about working with others, managing employees, and all aspects of running a compassionate business. These tidbits will stand me in good stead forever.

Although my dad has an office back here—littered with papers and invoices and sugar—I usually find him somewhere near the oven. Like a giant paddlewheel, the inside mechanism rotates long, narrow shelves so that everything bakes consistently. Trays upon trays can bake at the same time, and Dad knows when to take them out just by looking—he just knows when they're done.

One of the most practical features in this bakery is the set of cabinets that act as walls dividing the back and front of the bakery. The wooden backs can be slid shut, hiding the kitchen from the customers—but if they're open, then Dad can look

straight through the glass fronts, into the other cases. It's how he knows when to bring in another dozen molasses cookies, or three more loaves of rye.

From my privileged vantage points—either through those secret doors, or behind the front cases—I can see the customers through the display cases. In either case, I look through the heavy sliding glass door with the brass dimple for a fingerhold, between small stacks of cookies on trays.

I'm especially interested in seeing other kids. I like to watch them looking at me with mesmerized surprise and envy, wishing they could parade behind the cases, too, like that little girl. They stand there with only a piece of glass between them and all the cookies in the world.

One day, decades later, I stood up in a storytelling workshop on the island where I live. My first story has always been the bakery. So I told it. The bakery is my main character. As I weave the first telling, I realize that everything I have ever created came from the home that the bakery gave my family and me. My grandfather didn't tell family stories; he lived them. Baked them to life. The bakery was always his point of reference, my dad's point of reference, my point of reference. I found the archetypal story from which all my stories came, and I sang them.

I wrote my dad that night to tell him what had happened inside me. I told him how I identified The Story. I told him what

I remembered about the bakery, how all the hours he stood at those ovens—or at the work table, or sleeping on flour sacks—were not in vain. Not only did he put three daughters through college, but he also gave us beautiful homes to grow up in. And he nurtured an entire community. I told him that I knew it was his job to feed everyone, and that he thought he was baking and selling loaves of bread and boxes of cookies—but that he was handing out love. Sugarcoated diamonds. I wanted Dad to know all of this in case he happened to die in the night.

Even when I was little, I used to wake in the middle of the night and listen to him snore. I always knew that one day he wouldn't wake up, and for some reason I felt like his witness. It wasn't at all macabre or sad; it was just part of my day-to-day. Eventually, I expanded that awareness to all the people I cared about. I consciously told them I loved them, just in case I'd never see them again. Sometimes, in his sleep, Dad would hold one breath for so long that I would start to worry. I know now that it was probably just sleep apnea, but during those nights, I would wait, thinking surely I would hear mom screaming soon. Then the silence would be broken by a loud, gasping inhalation, and I would let my breath out, too.

On that storytelling night all those years later, I was not going to risk his not knowing that my heart had just put two and two together.

He had to know that I would share his recipes.

Above: Marcy and Max, having a quiet moment, shortly before I married my second husband.
Opposite: Another moment, less quiet, at Rehoboth Beach, Delaware, when I was about 8.

Dad,

I HAVE TO TELL YOU NOW – *tonight, before tomorrow comes!*

Today I told a certain story in front of an audience for the first time. The working title is "(I'm) A Baker's Daughter."

I told about every display case, about Rose and her Lifesavers, how you once decorated one whole side of a wedding cake in less than 15 minutes, and how you came home from the bakery every day with sugar all down your front.

How—somehow—loaves of bread put daughters through school, and fed a whole community And the Brenner family—aunts, uncles, your Mom and my Bubbe—showed their love by feeding people, passing down the milk and honey to you, Max, my father, my friend, my friendly witness. And you gave it to me. It is the best gift ever!

This story is so rich, and it has been in front of my face all along! It is my story and I'm going to write it. The bakery contains the whole story of me. A huge part of me always wanted to carry on the bakery. Maybe this is how.

I didn't want tomorrow to come without being sure that you know how much it all means to me and lives in my heart and soul—and how I want to pass the story of our family to others. I want to share your legacy. And your recipes. Brenner's Bakery has to live on.

We are lucky to have this story of love, family, community, and survival. Nothing matters more.

I love you so deep and true,
Marcy

A BAKER'S DAUGHTER

Hi Marcy,

I have not cried for a long time. This is a heartwarming letter you wrote, and it touched me deeply!

Thank you for being who you are!

Your life has been full of adventure and learning, but the utmost positive is your honesty and warmth!

The dark days you have lived through, the goodness in your soul, have been a rewarding part of your being!

I LOVE YOU!

Thank you for sending this wonderful story, I will treasure it forever!

Dad

Dad did not die that night. Tomorrow gratefully came, shining in the windows the next morning. Max got the email message and would know for the rest of his days.

Until I was about 22, I dreamed about running the bakery. As my sisters went into their chosen professions and lives, I nurtured a secret idea, to use my business degree to take the bakery into the 21st century—all the while bringing back the nostalgia of the bygone era of the bakery from the 1940s and 1950s. I wrote a whole marketing plan, complete with a logo of Big Bubbe delivering bread from a horse and buggy. I wanted to bring folks back to the neighborhood bakery shop—realizing that while we had to replicate everything Brenner's was known for, the heart of the bakery was its cookies. Bread was its sustenance, but cookies were its gateway drug. There were so many flavors—literally, something for everyone. Cookies went to home kitchens, schools, birthday and holiday parties, potlucks, slumber parties, picnics. Sometimes they didn't make it out of the bakery. They were easy to just pick up and eat right out of the box.

My dream had to change because of real life. My brother-in-law Harry Sherman began working with dad when I was just ten years old. By the time I was in college, our family bakery was naturally passed down to him. My next dream, the replacement dream, took me west for twenty years, and into music and marketing. But I still thought about a bakery. When I moved back east to the Outer Banks, I would see street corners that beckoned for one. For a while, I wondered if my destiny was to create a new little storefront sweets-and-bread shop.

As it turns out, I realized that the bakery represented my family's center—nurturing, home, togetherness—and that perhaps my expression of all of those things could be different. For example, my husband Lou and I make and share music, with our musical "family." That is one "bakery." This book is another.

CHOCOLATE TOP COOKIES

Although breads were a quietly consistent and important staple at Brenner's, the Chocolate Top Cookie—a Butter Cookie topped with Chocolate Fudge Icing—was the most popular item in the entire bakery. Everyone's favorite by far. The Chocolate Top got people excited.

It still does. Some of my childhood friends—who are now in their fifties—still sigh when they think about Chocolate Tops. The cookie itself is buttery and delicate, but still crunchy enough to hold the beautiful big drop of chocolate fudge icing. Because of its iconic status, I've detailed the Chocolate Top's entire process—how to make the cookie, how to make the icing, and how to form the "Top."

When working on this recipe, I knew the moment I had the icing right. I'd eaten one of these cookies—or two, or perhaps three—and my tongue discovered a tiny, lost piece of chocolate on my lip. As soon as it touched my taste buds, the flavor exploded in my mouth all over again. It flooded my mind with sense memories of the bakery, my childhood, my dad—all that was right in the world of a kid. That little bit of chocolate brought me right back to 1984, the last time I ate a Chocolate Top baked at Brenner's. I felt the texture and recognized how the icing behaved; I was home. Then I went to work perfecting the butter cookie.

I've been taking pictures of people in my village as I share samples of the Chocolate Top. No matter the tasters' ages or backgrounds, when people taste their first one, the same

thing happens. The icing is stacked high, so they have to really open their mouths—and then their eyebrows raise, their eyes look skyward, and they start laughing. With their mouths full. Happens every time.

There are a few ways to eat this delicious confection. Some people start by nibbling the butter cookie all the way around, then approach the rest with small bites of cookie paired with chocolate. Some lick all the chocolate off, and then tackle the cookie. I liked them best when the icing was still soft inside, but the chocolate surface was just set in a tender shiny crust. In this delicate state, they were too fresh to stack on top of one another. I'd eat it in three bites, equal parts cookie and icing.

And as they "age," Chocolate Tops take on characteristics I also recall—the chocolate forms a thin, hard crust, but retains a semisoft center. Meanwhile, the cookie loses crunch, but not flavor. Amazingly, even when completely stale, it's still a great cookie.

Note: Because the signature Chocolate Fudge Icing is used in many other recipes, it also is included in the cake chapter (page 142) and throughout the book, as needed.

CHOCOLATE TOP FINESSE

**Makes about
4 dozen cookies**
Butter Cookies (page 90)
Chocolate Fudge Icing (page 92)

Notes:
For Chocolate Tops, the ideal decorating tip is the #9 French Star, 11/16".

I keep a batch of Butter Cookies in the freezer and Chocolate Fudge Icing in the refrigerator for emergencies.

While patiently waiting for your batch of Butter Cookies to cool, whip up the Chocolate Fudge Icing. Once the cookies are completely (really, completely) cool, then prepare yourself to channel Max.

Using a piping bag, gently touch the top of each cookie with the tip. Squeeze a big dollop of fudge icing, remaining close to the cookie's surface. Let the icing fill out to ¼" from the edge (or whatever size drop you want). Then, still holding the tip close to the cookie, with a circular motion, twist and lift the tip straight up. (For more details on how to make and use a piping bag or decorating cone, see General Techniques, page 262.)

Alternately, it is possible to get a perfectly fine result by using a smaller star tip and circling around and up to form a nice dollop of icing. If you don't have any cake decorating supplies, then spoon a rounded glob and swirl it into shape. These will look different from Brenner's but will taste just like you remember.

BUTTER COOKIES

Butter cookies are delicate, slightly crunchy, and decorated in all sorts of ways. Yes, they form the foundation of the Chocolate Top Cookie, but we always thought of them as a bakery staple on their own. They're particularly great during the holidays, and especially as a Christmas treat—but the possibilities are endless.

**Makes about
4 dozen cookies**
4 c cake flour
(or all-purpose)
⅛ c milk powder
pinch salt
2½ c shortening
1½ c granulated sugar
1½ t vanilla extract
1 t butter flavor
¾ t almond extract
2 egg yolks
2 whole eggs

This is a delicate cookie. All-purpose flour produces a less delicate result—which I prefer—but you might try it both ways.

Whisk together flour, milk powder, and salt in a medium bowl; set aside. In another bowl—on low in standing mixer or by hand—cream together shortening, sugar, vanilla, butter flavor, and almond extract, scraping down sides and beater.

Beat egg yolks together with a fork; add to batter while mixing. Then add whole eggs one at a time, also while mixing batter for 30 seconds (on Level 1 with mixer), scraping sides between additions until well combined, creamy and fluffy.

Add flour mixture, ⅓ at a time, mixing for 30 seconds after each addition until smooth, scraping down sides and beater.

Chill dough for 2 hours or overnight. The dough will be sticky but still able to roll into balls. If too sticky, flour your hands or add a bit more flour to the dough—but not too much or cookie will be dry.

Note—About Butter:
I used shortening and butter flavor because the recipe said to—but also, see page 257 for more background.

Variations:
My favorites among the many identities of the butter cookie: the iconic Chocolate Top Cookie (page 86); and the short, piped, star-shaped, log cookies. The latter variety can be decorated with a dip of powdered sugar icing or chocolate fudge glaze on one half. Add sprinkles for extra flair.

Preheat oven to 325°F.

Roll dough into 1–1½" balls; arrange 1" apart on ungreased or parchment-lined cookie sheet. Using the bottom of a floured glass, gently press the balls flat until about ½" thick. Store unused portion in refrigerator while baking batches.

Note: These also can be hand-rolled into a short log shape, or piped, using a star-shaped tip (shown above right). If you want to pipe, don't refrigerate the dough. Or, if one batch comes out too stiff to pipe, next time use less flour and allow the dough to be just moist enough to pipe.

Bake until the bottom edges just start to turn color, about 14-16 minutes. Don't let them brown or over bake—unless you prefer a crunchier butter cookie.

Let cool on the baking sheet about 5 minutes before trying to remove (with a gentle twist) so they won't break. Let completely cool on a rack before icing or decorating.

THE BAKERY

CHOCOLATE FUDGE ICING & GLAZE

Mix all ingredients with a standing mixer or by hand until very smooth and just turns fluffy and spreadable. Let it stand a few minutes, give it a quick mix and then check again, as it may need a bit more liquid. Add more milk or water to adjust, a little at a time.

This recipe is the way I remember it, on the bittersweet side—but you can adjust the amount of sugar to desired sweetness. If you shift sugar quantities, you might have to add a bit more liquid, too. Note: sugar also shifts the color a bit.

The icing should be moist and soft enough to pipe, but still be very fudgy and firm enough to hold the drop shape on top of the Butter Cookie. The icing will set on the outside when dry, but stay moist inside, just like Brenner's.

Makes about a quart (32 oz., 2#)
1⅓ c chocolate fudge base (one 12-oz. container)
¾ t vanilla extract
6+ c powdered sugar (measure then sift)
¾+ c milk or water (don't use all at once)

Above: Max topping cookies at a Relay for Life event, where both authors snacked more than they walked.

Variation—Glaze
For Danishes, Doughnuts, Éclairs (and Brownies, if you like a thinner consistency):
Follow recipe above, gradually add about ¼ c more milk or water—as desired, for a more spreadable result. Glaze will not be stiff enough to make a piped or spooned shape.

About Fudge Base
Shhh: The secret of the Chocolate Top Cookie is the fudge base. If you want to make your own, there are many recipes available online. However, I get mine from a company that has been making it for more than 40 years. This base makes icing and glaze taste just like Brenner's. Tell them I sent you!

Source for Fudge Base:
Party Time
3350 Bluebonnet Blvd., Baton Rouge, LA 70809
(225) 927-3270
partytimebr.com, or
contact@partytimebr.com

THE BAKERY

SUGAR COOKIES

My sisters and I loved these cookies any which way—granulated sugar on top was the regular version, but for holidays they were iced.

Makes about 3 dozen cookies
- 3 c cake flour (or all-purpose)
- 3½ t baking powder
- 1 T powdered milk
- 1½ t salt
- 1¼ c shortening
- 2 c granulated sugar
- 1 T vanilla extract
- 3 eggs

PREPARATION

In a mixing bowl, combine flour, milk powder, baking powder, and salt; set aside. In another bowl, cream shortening and sugar together until light and fluffy, scraping sides of bowl and beater. Add vanilla and mix until combined.

Alternate by adding one egg at a time with portions of the flour mixture until all eggs and flour are combined and the dough is smooth. Scrape sides of bowl and beater between additions. Cover and refrigerate for at least 2 hours; overnight is great.

Preheat oven to 325°F.

Line cookie sheet with parchment paper or lightly grease. The next step depends on which variation you choose.

SHAPING OR CUTOUTS

For traditional cookies, use rounded teaspoons or a scoop to place 1½" balls of dough directly onto cookie sheet, 1" apart. With a floured rolling pin, the bottom of a glass, or a hand, press cookies down to ¼–½".

For cutout shapes, place dough on a lightly floured board or surface, and with floured hands and rolling pin, roll out ⅓ of the dough to desired thickness. Brenner's standard was about ½" thick—thinner will be crunchier than Brenner's. Use a cookie cutter of choice—or a glass to make a circle—and arrange on a cool baking sheet 1" apart. A spatula works well for lifting the delicate shapes off the rolling/cutting surface and onto the baking sheet without breaking. Simple shapes work best.

THE BAKERY

FINISHING

If you want decorations baked in, which increases the sweetness quotient, then sprinkle adornments first—try granulated white or colored sugar, sprinkles, or other favorites. If you prefer less built-in sweetness, then add decoration after baking; if you prefer double sweetness, add before and after. (I recycle a spice bottle with holes to apply plain sugar decoration.)

Put remaining dough in the refrigerator while baking batches.

BAKING / COOLING

Bake trays for about 11–14 minutes, depending on thickness of the cookie. Allow to bake only until bottom edge just begins to turn brown. Do not over bake.

To avoid breakage, wait until cookie cools on baking sheet until firmed up, about 5 minutes; then place on a cooling rack.

Cookies can be iced when completely cool. If kept in a cool spot, the icing will set up enough to allow cookies to touch after about 30 minutes.

Powdered Sugar Drizzle/Icing
6+ c powdered sugar (measure then sift)
⅓ c milk or water (might need less; add a little at a time)
⅛ c (2 T) vanilla extract

Mix ingredients. To achieve a light icing consistency, you might need a bit less liquid; add slowly until it's perfect.

Chocolate Fudge Icing
Makes about a quart (32 oz., 2#)
1⅓ c chocolate fudge base (one 12-oz. container; see page 93)
¾ t vanilla extract
6+ c powdered sugar (measure then sift)
¾+ c milk or water (don't use all at once)

Mix ingredients until very smooth and fluffy. Let stand a few minutes; check consistency and adjust liquid.

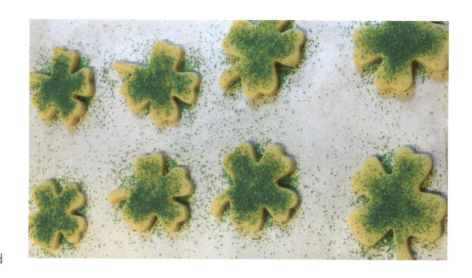

ICING / DECORATING
Of course, you can do about a million things with a batch of Sugar Cookies and pots of icing. The bakery made holidays special with these cookies, and I can give you a few examples of our standards. But really: get creative.

Halloween
Round "pumpkins" iced completely with orange Powdered Sugar (Drizzle) Icing. After it set, we added Chocolate Fudge Icing for the eyes and mouth of a Jack-O-Lantern face.

Christmas
A candy cane shape from plain (white) Powdered Sugar Icing with red and green piped icing stripes.

St. Patrick's Day
A clover leaf shape with green granulated sugar.

THE BAKERY

CHOCOLATE CHIP COOKIES

In my humble Brenner opinion, this Chocolate Chip cookie is simply the best chocolate chip cookie ever—with a perfect combination of crunchy and chewy, and a wonderful pecan aftertaste. When I was a kid and these went stale, all I had to do was put one in the microwave for a few seconds and it was fresh again. Heaven. And when I started my recipe re-creation, this recipe produced the best cookie I've ever had, right out of the shoot.

Makes about 3-4 dozen cookies

- 2 c cake flour (or all-purpose)
- 2¼ t salt
- 1½ t baking soda
- 1⅓ c shortening
- 1½ c brown sugar
- ¾ c granulated sugar
- 2 eggs
- 1½ t vanilla extract
- 2 c chocolate chips (12-oz. package)
- ¾ c chopped pecans (chop, then measure)

Combine flour, salt, and soda in a mixing bowl; set aside. In another bowl—either standing mixer or by hand—cream shortening until very smooth. Then add sugars and cream until smooth and light, scraping the beater and sides of bowl.

Add eggs to batter, one at a time. Cream together until fluffy with each addition, for a minute or less, scraping sides of bowl and beater. Add vanilla and blend.

Add dry ingredient mixture ⅓ at a time, blending on low or by hand with each addition until smooth, scraping sides and beater. Stir in pecans and chocolate chips; mix until combined.

Although the dough is very sticky, it bakes up fine. If you'd like it less sticky, then refrigerate for a few hours or even overnight.

Preheat oven to 325°F.

Roll or scoop dough into 2" balls, place about 2" apart on an ungreased or parchment-lined cookie sheet.

Bake until golden brown, about 17–19 minutes, then let cool a few minutes before transferring to a cooling rack.

OATMEAL RAISIN COOKIES

Molasses is the first "surprise" ingredient in this cookie; it provides the distinctive flavor and chewiness. When I mixed the dough for the first time, the sharp, tangy smell of molasses transported me to my dad's side in the bakery. The other surprise is chopped raisins. The bakery ingredient card called for ground raisins, but chopped more closely resembled my memory. And don't cheat. By processing the raisins, you allow their flavor to permeate the cookie. Believe me, these taste different if you use whole raisins.

Makes about 4 dozen cookies

4½ c cake flour (or all-purpose)
1 T salt
1 T baking soda
1½ t cinnamon
1½ c shortening
1⅔ c brown sugar
1⅔ c granulated sugar
¼ c molasses
4 eggs
1¼ c old-fashioned rolled oats
½ c raisins (chopped, firmly packed)

Combine flour, salt, soda, and cinnamon in mixing bowl; set aside. In another bowl—either standing mixer or by hand—cream shortening, then add sugars and molasses; mix together until smooth and light, scraping the beater and sides of bowl.

Add eggs to batter, one at a time. Cream together until fluffy with each addition, for a minute or less, scraping sides and beater.

Add the dry ingredient mixture and blend on low until smooth, scraping sides of bowl and beater.

Stir in oats and raisins and mix until combined. It will be a little sticky, but that's perfect. No need to refrigerate, but if you don't want to bake the entire batch, you can cover and refrigerate this dough. Bring to room temperature before shaping/baking.

Note: These cookies make wonderful ice cream sandwiches. Dad and I would use vanilla ice cream but any flavor works. Spoon slightly softened ice cream about 1½″ thick between two cookies. Wrap individually in wax paper or baggie, place all in an air-tight plastic bag, and freeze.

Preheat oven to 325°F.

Make 2″ balls of dough, place about 2″ apart on a lightly greased or parchment-lined cookie sheet. Using the floured bottom of a glass, press the top flat to about ½″ thick.

Brush with Egg Wash (page 276).

Bake until deep golden brown, about 17–19 minutes, then let cool a few minutes before transferring to a cooling rack. With this cookie, a minute more or less changes the texture from chewier (less time) to crunchier (more time). In my kitchen, 18 minutes is perfect—chewy with a crunchy edge.

OATMEAL CHOCOLATE CHIP COOKIES

These Oatmeal Chocolate Chip cookies have a distinctive flavor, and a sublime aftertaste. I could sense it from the back of my nose and into my sinuses when I was mixing the first batch. I couldn't have described that to you until I made this recipe.

The "eureka!" for this cookie...cinnamon.

Makes about 3–4 dozen cookies
3 c cake flour (or all-purpose)
2⅛ t cinnamon
1 T salt
1½ t baking soda
¾ c brown sugar
1⅔ c granulated sugar
1⅔ c shortening
3 eggs
1 T vanilla extract
1¾ c old-fashioned rolled oats
2 c chocolate chips (12-oz. package)

Combine flour, cinnamon, salt, and soda in a medium bowl; set aside In another bowl—either standing mixer or by hand—cream sugars and shortening until light and fluffy.

Add eggs to creamed mixture one at a time. Cream together until fluffy with each addition, for a minute or less, scraping sides of bowl and beater. Add vanilla; cream together until smooth and light, again scraping the beater and bowl.

Add the dry ingredient mixture, ⅓ at a time, blending on low until smooth with each addition, scraping sides and beater. Add oats and chocolate chips, and mix until combined. Dough will be stiff and sticky.

Preheat oven to 325°F.

Using rounded 1T scoops of dough, roll into 2" balls, place about 2" apart on an ungreased or parchment-lined cookie sheet. Dough will be sticky, but still should roll into a ball. However, if too sticky, refrigerate for 30 minutes. Use the bottom of a floured glass to press cookies to about ½" in thickness.

Bake until golden brown, about 17–19 minutes, then let cool for a few minutes before transferring them to a cooling rack.

COCONUT CHOCOLATE CHIP COOKIES

**Makes about
3-4 dozen cookies**
3 c cake flour
(or all-purpose)
pinch of salt
1¾ c shortening
1¾ c granulated sugar
3 eggs
1 T vanilla extract
1 t almond extract
1¾ c shredded coconut
(lightly packed)
2 c chocolate chips
(12-oz. package)

Combine flour and salt in a mixing bowl; set aside. In another bowl—standing mixer or by hand—cream shortening and sugar until light and fluffy.

Add eggs to batter one at a time. Cream together until fluffy with each addition, for a minute or less, scraping sides of bowl and beater. Add vanilla and almond extract; cream together until smooth and light, again scraping the sides and beater.

On low setting (or by hand), add the dry ingredient mixture, ⅓ at time, mixing after each addition until combined. Mix until smooth, scraping sides and beater. Add coconut and chocolate chips; mix until combined. Dough will be sticky.

Variation—Pecan Sandies

Remove coconut and chocolate chips from the list, then add the following ingredients. The process is the same!

1½ pecans (chopped then measured)
½ c extra flour
½ t extra salt

Preheat oven to 325°F.

Roll into 1½" balls, and place about 1" apart on an ungreased or parchment-lined cookie sheet.

Bake until just brown on the edge, about 17-19 minutes, then let cool for a few minutes before transferring to a cooling rack.

THE BAKERY

MOLASSES COOKIES

This is an extraordinary cookie, and for many, a favorite. These large, dark brown circles coated with a thick layer of granulated sugar, were usually packed in little square stacks of two dozen in a plastic bag. We piled these bags on the counter—at the intersection of cookies and pies—where they'd sell out immediately.

The Molasses Cookie has a couple of unusual ingredients. The first is baking ammonia. Also known as ammonium bicarbonate, this ingredient was used before the existence of baking soda and baking powder. When heated, baking ammonia breaks down into ammonia (NH_3), water, and carbon dioxide. The carbon dioxide makes cakes and cookies rise, the same way that carbon dioxide given off by other chemical leaveners does. Bakers who are familiar with baking ammonia—and have substituted baking soda to compare—find that ammonia makes recipes much lighter. When I was little, the ammonia would sting my eyes and the inside of my nose when I peeked over the edge of the big, silver Hobart mixing bowl. Now, as a grown-up—and tall enough that my nose is out of range—that isn't what I'm thinking about.

What I am thinking about is the second unusual ingredient. "Crumbs" referred to all of the day-old goodies, which were dumped into the mixer right off the display trays, out of plastic

bags, and off cardboard cake circles, all tipped into the ammonia-smelling mix. Dad would let me put the crumbs in while he weighed out the other ingredients. It is still a mystery how all those items could be tossed in—cakes with buttercream and whipped cream icing, pastry with fruit or cheese filling, pies—and still the Molasses cookies looked, tasted, and maintained the same texture. Every time.

When I first tried this recipe by myself, I placed into my little Kitchen Aide mixer the flour, sugar, ammonia, soda, salt, molasses; all the ingredients on the ingredient card, with the exception of the crumbs. Instead, I added flour until I had what I hoped would be the right consistency. It ended up requiring 2 cups more flour than I imagined, making the recipe too large. I had to recalculate and try again.

"You just add crumbs until it's right," Dad said, when I asked him how to make the dough—when the "day-olds" were different for every batch. Like the production "list" he and Rose would make every Monday, he just knew. It's a sweet mystery wrapped up in genes, intuition, and lots of time.

THE BAKERY

Makes about 5 dozen
6 c cake flour
(or all-purpose)
1 T baking soda
1 T powdered ammonia
½ t allspice
1½ c shortening
1½ c granulated sugar
3 c molasses
½+ c granulated sugar
(in small bowl, set aside)

Combine flour, soda, ammonia, and allspice in a medium mixing bowl. Note: if you're a fan of drier cookies, then add ½ c flour.

In a separate bowl—standing mixer or by hand—beat shortening until smooth, about a minute. Add 1½ c sugar and beat until well combined and smooth, about 2 minutes. Add molasses and mix until combined. Gradually add dry ingredients until well blended.

Preheat oven to 325°F.

Roll 2T scoops of dough into 2" balls; roll half of each one in the additional granulated sugar, leaving the other half un-coated.

Place on a lightly greased or parchment-lined baking sheet 2" apart, sugar side up. Using a drinking glass or your hand, press each ball down to a ½"-thick disk. Don't be afraid to really press it down to that thickness, otherwise it could be too fudgy in the middle. Refrigerate remaining dough between batches.

Bake for 14–16 minutes; bottoms will be dark brown when done.

Optional: After cooling for five minutes, sprinkle additional granulated sugar after cooling.

Note: This cookie is even better on the second day! If you use the recipe without the additional ½ c of flour, they'll be fudgier on the first day and less fudgy on the second day.

Ammonia tip:
I order Powdered Ammonia from King Arthur Flour www.kingarthurflour.com.

THE BAKERY

PEANUT BUTTER COOKIES

The crisscross pattern on these sublime cookies provides more than a cute finish—it pushes the dough down, which allows the cookie to stay chewy inside—and crunchy on the outside and edges. They melt in your mouth.

Makes about 4 dozen cookies

2⅔ c cake flour (or all-purpose)
1½ t salt
1½ t baking soda
1¼ c brown sugar
1¼ c shortening
1¼ c granulated sugar
1⅛ c peanut butter
1½ t vanilla extract
3 eggs
⅓ c granulated sugar (for the finish)

In a mixing bowl, whisk together flour, salt and soda; set aside. In another bowl—standing mixer or by hand—cream together shortening, sugars, and peanut butter until smooth and light, scraping the beater and sides of bowl.

Add vanilla. Then add eggs one at a time. Cream together until fluffy with each addition, for a minute or less, scraping sides of bowl and beater.

Add the dry ingredient mixture ⅓ at a time, blending after each part, and blend on low until smooth, scraping sides and beater.

Preheat oven to 325°F.

Roll or scoop dough into 1½–2" balls and place about 2" apart on an ungreased or parchment-lined cookie sheet.

A BAKER'S DAUGHTER

Pressing ¼" deep, make a crisscross pattern in each cookie with a wide-prong fork, potato masher, or pastry knife. In the process, you'll push the dough down to about half the height of the ball. Sprinkle with the ⅓ c granulated sugar.

Bake until golden brown, about 16–18 minutes, then let cool a few minutes before transferring them to a cooling rack—making sure to lift with a gentle twist. The cookie will have a crunchy edge and chewy center, just like you remember!

THE BAKERY

GINGERBREAD COOKIES

Makes 2 dozen cut-outs
3½ c cake flour
(or all-purpose)
½ t salt
1½ t baking soda
¾ t dry ground ginger
pinch ground cloves
(or allspice)
½ c shortening
¾ c brown sugar
½ c molasses
2 eggs
2 T raisins
(optional, for decoration)

Combine flour, salt, soda, and spices in a mixing bowl; set aside. In another bowl—standing mixer or by hand—cream shortening, then add sugar and molasses; cream together until smooth and light, scraping sides of bowl and beater.

Add eggs one at a time. Cream together until fluffy with each addition, for a minute or less, scraping sides of bowl and beater.

Add the dry ingredient mixture, ⅓ at a time, blending on low after each addition until smooth, scraping sides and beater.

Preheat oven to 325°F.

Working with half the dough at a time (refrigerate the remainder), place dough on a well-floured surface. Using a floured rolling pin, roll out to ¼" thick. Re-flour your surface/roller as needed so cutouts won't stick.

Using floured cookie cutter, cut out shapes—Gingerbread Person or any other. Using a spatula to keep them from breaking, place on a lightly oiled or parchment-lined baking sheet 1" apart.

For "buttons" and/or "eyes" use raisins (or any cookie decoration) pressed lightly into the cutout.

Bake about 9–11 minutes, then let cool 5 minutes on the baking sheet before gently twisting them with the spatula and carefully transferring to a cooling rack.

THE BAKERY

ICEBOX COOKIES

Combine flour and salt in a medium bowl; set aside. In another bowl—standing mixer or by hand—cream shortening until very smooth, about 1–2 minutes. Add powdered sugar and vanilla; cream until smooth and light, scraping sides and beater.

Add eggs one at a time. Cream together until fluffy with each addition, for a minute or less, scraping sides of bowl and beater.

Add the dry ingredient mixture, $1/3$ at a time. After each addition, blend on low or by hand until smooth, scraping sides and beater.

Take out a little less than half the dough and place into a medium bowl. Stir in cocoa powder until combined.

Refrigerate all dough for at least 2 hours in the separate bowls—but if you're in a hurry, put it in the freezer, but don't let it freeze. When dough is chilled, you'll make two logs of swirled dough.

For each flavor—vanilla and chocolate—follow the same process. Cut dough in half. Place one half back in its bowl in the refrigerator, and the other half onto a cookie sheet-sized piece of parchment or plastic wrap. Cover with another piece of parchment or plastic wrap and roll out to rectangle shapes, no more than $1/4$" thickness. Place in the refrigerator. You'll have four dough rectangles, two of each flavor. The vanilla rectangles will be larger than the chocolate ones.

Chill rectangles of dough for 2 hours or more. You can place them in the freezer—just briefly, though. Don't let them freeze.

Makes about 3–4 dozen
4 c cake flour
(or all-purpose)
1 ⅛ t salt
3 c shortening
3 ⅓ c powdered sugar
1 T vanilla extract
4 eggs
½ c cocoa powder

For each log: Take the top sheet off both of the chilled rectangles. As you place the chocolate half (smaller) on top of the vanilla half, also peel away the other parchment/plastic sheet. Roll the resulting sandwich of dough from its longer end, forming a long, narrow log. As you go, carefully peel off the bottom layer of parchment/plastic. Cover the finished log with parchment, tuck in the sides, and place in refrigerator overnight. Again, you can pop these logs in the freezer—just briefly, though. Don't freeze.

When ready to bake, preheat oven to 325°F.

Place one chilled log of dough onto a surface or board. Open the parchment paper, exposing the whole roll. Cut ¼–½" thick circles from the log with a sharp knife, placing them 1" apart on a parchment-lined or ungreased cookie sheet.

Bake until just turning brown on the bottom outer edge, about 10–12 minutes, then let cool a few minutes before transferring to a cooling rack.

THE BAKERY

FRUIT BARS

Makes about 24 squares.
2 c raisins (whole)
1 c shredded coconut (sweetened)
1¼ c cake flour (or all-purpose)
1¼ t salt
⅜ t baking soda
1¾ t baking power
½ c shortening
1 c granulated sugar
1 egg, lightly beaten
½ c honey
¾ t vanilla extract

In a large bowl, combine raisins and coconut; set aside. In another bowl, whisk together flour, salt, baking soda, and baking powder; set aside

In a third bowl—standing mixer or by hand—beat shortening until fluffy. Add sugar; beat until combined and fluffy, about a minute, scraping sides and beater. Add egg, honey and vanilla; blend until smooth.

Add flour, salt, baking soda, and baking powder mixture to the wet ingredients. Mix until smooth, about 2 minutes, scraping sides and beater.

Gently fold in the raisin and coconut mixture until well combined.

Preheat oven to 350°F.

Spread dough into a parchment-lined half baking sheet (13" x 18") all the way out to the edges, as evenly as possible.

Bake at 350°F for 25–28 minutes until golden brown.

Allow to fully cool, then cut into squares.

THE BAKERY

CHAPTER 4
THE WHISTLER

Max whistled so much that his lips were slightly, permanently puckered, and firm when he pecked me on the lips. Wherever he was, I could find him by tracking his whistle, along with the jingle of change in his pockets. I just had to listen—in the bakery, the house, the yard. Even now, when I conjure him, these sounds come to the forefront, from a deep place in my brain. When I was first working on this project, and Dad and I were talking a lot, working on recipes, I noticed that I whistle, too. Eventually, I realized that we both went around our days, whistling little sound tracks, bits of tunes—but I had never noticed it until I was hanging around with him, being conscious of whistling. I realize that we were both like parrots. I watched how it worked with Max: Whatever he heard, he whistled back.

Mom always said that Dad whistled when he was angry. "What? Noooo," I said, assuming that she was just misinterpreting him. I was always confounded by this idea, because his whistling was ever present—and if he did it only when he was mad, well then, he had always been mad. And that didn't describe him at all. I once asked my nephew, Jason Sherman, who had worked in the back with all the guys. "Nana said that Pop-Pop whistled when he was angry." I said it with a skeptical and dismissing tone, leading the witness. I was shocked when he said, "Oh yeah. For sure. You knew if he was mad, if something had gotten messed up." But then as we talked, we both agreed that he whistled all the time, in all conditions, so it was something bigger. I've decided it was self-soothing. He whistled to stay calm, centered, and focused.

Dad's whistling helped everyone around him to stay calm, too. Jason said it worked, that his Pop-Pop's whistling soothed everyone in the bakery, like a balm of love. Like hot chocolate on a cold day, or lemonade in the summer sun. It was whatever you needed it to be. Thankfully, he was a really good whistler, too. (Wouldn't it have been terrible for all those people, for all those years, if he hadn't been?) The songs he whistled were the songs that got stuck in his head. He played them over and over, maybe a song from the radio or a TV show that he'd heard. He whistled it until another one took its place. I asked Jason if it got to be bothersome, hearing the same one again and again. He said, surprisingly, no. It was soothing for everyone.

The repetition helped me to learn about music; it was like practicing scales. I learned "Stormy Weather" on a day when I was in the back with the guys. It was pouring outside.

As a musician, I call them "ear worms"—the songs that get stuck in my head. In my experience, the only cure for an ear worm is to sing it, play it—or whistle it. Processing a song through my fingers or breath shifts the melody through me and out again; it transforms the feeling of the song into something tangible and sends it on its way. I believe that while Dad "whistled while he worked," he also connected to his breath. Whistling, like singing, put to bed angst or frustration or fear.

A SWEET MISSION

Dad meant to create a bakery, but he created a community, both inside and outside the bakery. He did it by just doing his job, by making the food we all use to mark occasions. And while he looked upon his profession as his duty to his family, he also took pleasure from it. His favorite thing was to give a kid a cookie—or, really, whatever she wanted. For example, on summer evenings, I would hear the sound of the ice cream truck's tinny, recorded jingle. I'd search out his whistle and slip my hand into the pocket of his white work pants, still dusted with sugar and dried icing, for a handful of coins. If there was enough to go around, he always let me buy a Popsicle or Good Humor bar for one of the neighborhood kids, too. My favorite was the chocolate éclair or strawberry shortcake, with the crunchies.

And the next morning, every morning except Mondays, Dad would get up at 3 a.m. and drive to the bakery. We wouldn't see him again until late afternoon or even dinner time. Each day, he was greeted by a mountain of dough that had proofed—bakery-talk for "risen"—overnight. Then, all day long, he stood at the big rotating oven. From that vantage point, he periodically peered through the back of the cases to see what needed replenishing, what needed to be baked next. He filled those front cases six days a week, fifty weeks a year, for forty-three years.

He did his job, fed his family, and had a life—one dozen cookies, one loaf of bread at a time.

Max doing his thing at the bakery, circa 1950s.

A BAKER'S DAUGHTER

Max baked enough to put his three girls through school. He bought his wife all the clothes she could ever want and a grand house on the riverfront—our friends loved to play in the pool or water ski off the back of the boat. Mom worked, too, after we were all in school, but my dad's unstoppable, unquestioned dedication formed and remains my example of a business. He showed me how something small, done over and over, creates something big. Something important. And the bakery gave him purpose. It was his birthright. It was in his genetic code, inherited from a similar dedication, from his father. The bakery sustained our lives as it had our ancestors' lives.

Like Big Bubbe, Dad was fond of his customers, and he loved to see them happy, but his time was best spent with the process of baking. Not talking. When a gap appeared in the display cases, Dad would quickly step to the front, pop in a fresh tray, and retreat back through the swinging door. On one hand, he usually had something baking in the oven and had to get back to it. On the other hand, each customer represented an entire family, and also that day's particular story—Joey's birthday, Carlene's upcoming wedding—and there was too much to say. Therefore, Max remained a rare bird, a White-Breasted Whistler who avoided eye contact. From the customers' point of view, a "Max sighting" was a rare and wonderful thing. Wishing for more of him, they often would call out, "Hi, Mr. Brenner!" or "Hello Max! How are you today?" He'd slip the pastel plastic

tray into the case, wave his hand, say, "Hi, fine, thank you," and then disappear into a cloud of fairy dust. I would watch the customers' faces as the door swung shut behind him. Even that fleeting connection left them feeling like they had had a whole conversation. He was contagious.

Rose Wetzel, Geneva Fuller, and Ruby Hoffman were his main line of defense in the front. They'd worked in that same location before the bakery belonged to my dad. The ladies-in-the-front wore white nurse-style uniforms and shoes, with hose; their hair was up in nets; they always had a cigarette burning in the big ashtray they stashed under the counter. It was a large, ceramic dish, full of spent cigarette ends, each branded with red lipstick. In today's world, we can't imagine having people smoke in a setting like that, but those were different times. Everyone smoked, in the front and back, and Max was famous for letting people be who they were. He wasn't about to criticize—and, truth be told, he was known to sneak a butt himself. The ladies, however, maintained their own code of decorum for the public. Not one customer saw a cigarette, and somehow—I can't imagine how—the bakery smelled like a bakery. My sense memory of the breads and sweets is not tinged with a scent of smoke—which either speaks to the power of sugar or the power of time.

Rose also had a secret weapon. She kept a Lifesaver—the milky, translucent, white kind with red spiraling through—perched precariously on the back of her tongue. She said it kept

Max with his "right-hand woman," Rose—a fixture at the bakery for decades.

her breath fresh, but I worried that she would choke on it. She was Dad's right-hand person for years, and closed the bakery at 9:00 p.m. every night. Besides my mother, she was the last person to talk to him each evening, calling the house to make "the list" for the bakers the next day. Rose would tell him what was left in the cases, and he would dictate the baking inventory. They never used any numbers or records to prepare the list; it just came from their experience—and the weather, holidays, and seasons. To me it was a magic trick.

SUPER POWERS

Meanwhile, Dad had secret weapon of his own. Discovering it was like discovering that Clark Kent is Superman—when Clark Kent is also your dad. It happened at the cake-decorating station, which was accessed through the left swivel door, between the phone and the bread case. The wooden decorating table always held a spool of deli paper in a black metal frame. The paper was used to make cone-shaped icing holders, the pointy ends of which either accommodated metal tips or were cut in shapes. The decorator could make beads, stems, lettering, or more elaborate shapes like leaves, flowers, and baby booties. On a normal day, several cones were loaded and ready, each with a different color.

Borders and scallops were applied to an iced cake with the help of a heavy, stainless, electric cake stand. When switched on, it hummed and spun. Roses were made separately, on a small, flat

metal disk, using a slanted tip. The decorator would create them petal by petal, starting with the middle, tilting and twirling the disk by its nail-like handle as the flower took shape. He used a pair of scissors to lift each soft icing bloom off the disk and place it on the cake. All the decorators worked so fast, it was like a time-lapse cartoon. The one I knew best—the main decorator during my childhood—was Bob. He would let me sit on a high stool next to the five-gallon buckets of butter cream icing as he worked. With a cigarette always hanging from his mouth, he patiently answered my endless stream of questions, and listened to my chatter.

Of course, I knew that Dad could decorate a cake with the best of them—but I didn't realize he was Superman until one scorching July day, when I went along with him on a delivery. We loaded a large, three-tiered wedding cake into the back of the bakery station wagon. On the way to the wedding at Ft. Belvoir Officer's Club, we made a quick stop at the grocery store—and when we come back out, the sun had melted half the cake's icing down into the wheel well. I didn't say one word as we raced back to the bakery. I sat silently on that stool and watched him redecorate that cake, white roses and all, in less than fifteen minutes, whistling all the while. He didn't miss a beat.

It was then that I first realized that Max was a man, a person with a skill. The bakery wasn't there for my amusement, or for his. The bakery was there because my dad knew what he was doing. I'd

Above: Me using the same cake spinner that Dad used at the bakery for all those years.
Opposite page: Max making a decorating cone from parchment paper.

A BAKER'S DAUGHTER

just watched him take his guitar solo. I'd seen him carry the ball down the field for the touchdown. He'd done it calmly, knowing that freaking out would not help him solve the problem. He was a craftsman, a professional—and he truly loved making those roses. Later, I would realize that decorating cakes was his primary creative outlet. It was fun for him to make the little birds, flowers, leaves, and blue or pink baby booties. He wrote people's names and best wishes. He might not have spent time in conversations in the front of the bakery, but he gave his heart to those decorations. He said what he needed to say through his hands.

    I learned a lot that day, in those fifteen minutes. I learned that getting upset wouldn't have helped, and that practicing makes a difference. It allows you to make the clutch play. It allows you to please the customer, without making a fuss.

    Years would pass until I also understood what he truly gave as a father. Sure, everyone who knew him confirms that Max was mostly magic—but he could have been magic and spent his few off-hours watching TV. Instead, he would come inside after his fifteen-hour day and let my friends and me drag him downstairs to watch our skits or dance routines. Or he would clatter baking pans down the stairs when we were huddled on the couch, watching scary movies. Way past his own bedtime, he would tuck us in by slowly creaking the door and saying, "Ooooooo."

    That cool basement was my creative space. Mom often had to send him down there to fetch me for dinner, when I was absorbed

Andrea Ricci giving me a guitar lesson with my pawn-shop guitar—in the basement where I used to get preoccupied with music.

in writing or playing music. I would have answered several of her calls with, "I'll be right up," but when she lost patience, she would send Dad—with his belt, to get my attention. He would gently descend those stairs, still in his white bakery clothes, and plead, "Baby, please come up for dinner!" He'd be smiling, since we both knew he would never hit me with that belt. I would realize I'd put him in a terrible position, so we would both scamper right up to the kitchen, trying not to crack up.

Once nephew Jason and I sorted out Dad's whistling habit, I reconsidered the few times I ever witnessed Max's anger. Upon reflection, Jason was right. You could tell Dad's feelings by kind of song he chose, and the quality of the whistle. It would get louder, and his countenance would get quieter. The difference was subtle. And the whistling always brought him back to center.

I remember only one time when my father ever disciplined me. It was during dinner—one of the few times when he never whistled. I was about four years old, and had just learned how to blow spit-bubbles. I decided to do that while sitting at the dinner table with my family. I was fascinated with my new skill.

Dad said, "Don't do that, baby," but I couldn't stop. It was such a fun skill to have. I kept doing it. I remember doing it.

"I said, stop blowing bubbles at the table!" he said again.

I could tell he was getting annoyed, especially since he was being so direct. This was serious business. I compulsively kept on. I couldn't help myself.

A BAKER'S DAUGHTER

My favorite cupcake, yellow cake with vanilla icing and multicolor sprinkles, was waiting in front of me on a little plate until I finished dinner. In a blur, Dad reached across our round oak dining table, turned that cupcake over on its sprinkles, and drew his fist down on the wax-paper bottom, smashing it right there in front of me. I was crushed, realizing that what Superman giveth, he could take away. I never disobeyed him, ever again.

Perhaps Dad's most potent super power was his signature whistle, the one he used to announce his arrival home. It was a sing-songy and lilting "Woooo-hoooo" that called any children in the house—we came running to see what he had in the little white box that day. "How soft is the icing on the brownies?" I'd ask. "Are there any cupcakes left?" Any dogs we had also came running. They loved him as much as we did—and not only because they got to lick his shoes.

On Sundays he got home early to start his short Monday weekend. Those were fresh-doughnut days. We looked for jelly filled, glazed, French crullers, old-fashioned cake, chocolate covered, sugary twists, or my favorite, anything with sprinkles.

I was born into a family of doers. The heritage of hard work had steeped into my family from those who escaped Jewish persecution and came to the land of milk and honey. My example of productivity has always been activity, but it was steady activity. No unnecessary rushing around—everybody just kept going, day after day, loaf after loaf.

THE WHISTLER

In fact, it was odd to see my dad move fast. His pocket change really rattled if he caught a ball, or tickled us. I remember that sound when he once rushed into the mud room, thinking I was choking. It was the day I learned how to whistle with a blade of grass pulled tight between my thumbs. That odd, wheezy sound, scared him, and he startled me, "What's going on in here!?" I grinned at him, discounting the worry on his face, thinking about how funny he looked moving that fast, and at how loud he jingled.

To my family, my "steady activity" went in the opposite direction. To them, it looked as if I were sitting still. I'm the only artist in the bunch, and my parents didn't understand how hours up in my room writing songs and strumming a guitar were productive. Although my process worked for me, I felt like I was sneaking around if I wasn't up on my feet, accomplishing. I still struggle with this every day. Sitting still. Deciding what's truly productive, not based on physical activity, but on results.

But I had no trouble embracing my father's primary language. All of my friends, throughout our lives, would quote him. We still do. "How about a piece of cake? A bologna sandwich, glass of milk?" The cake was always first, and we could always have it first. His cake was a personification of him. It meant that stopping for a moment was okay. Put your feet up, take it easy. It meant that whatever was happening—a regular day, a funeral, a final exam, a gymnastics tournament—would be sweeter. For Max, there was always time for cake. There was always room for cake.

When I want to feel connected to my dad, I have a slice of cake. I also think of Lauren Bacall in *To Have and Have Not*. "You just put your lips together and blow." Anywhere I go, at any time of day, when I hear a whistle, it calms me. Even though I know that a given whistler isn't Max, I associate the sound with patience and resilience. This is true even though I realize that the whistler might be having a very different sort of experience. Maybe that concert hall stage manager, who's setting up when we're on tour, is three hours behind. Maybe that invisible person in my island's grocery store, a few aisles over, is choosing food for a funeral. I can't help it. I feel a joyful calm wash over me when I hear them. That's how Max taught me to hear.

I hear love, whistling past the baked beans and amplifiers.

Max's Central High School football portraits, circa 1945, Washington, DC.

THE WHISTLER

YELLOW POUND CAKE

**Makes two, 8 ½"
(1 pound) loaves, or
two 8" rounds, or one
half-sheet, or about
24 cupcakes**
3 c cake flour
(measure then sift)
1 T salt
¾ t baking powder
⅛ c (2 T) milk powder
1½ c shortening
3 c granulated sugar
6 eggs (large)
1 c cold water
1 T vanilla extract
If desired: 1 t of almond,
orange, or lemon extract,
or zest of ½ lemon

Bring all ingredients to room temperature, except water. Grease and flour the pan(s). Preheat oven to 350°F.

In a medium bowl, sift together flour, salt, baking powder, and milk powder; set aside. In another bowl—either standing mixer or by hand—beat shortening so it's light and fluffy, about 30 seconds.

Gradually add sugar to the shortening, one cup at a time, beating 30 seconds after each addition (1–2 minutes total). Scrape sides of bowl and beater.

Add eggs one at a time, beating only enough to incorporate after each one (1–2 minutes total). Scrape sides of bowl and beater.

Add vanilla (and other flavors as desired); mix until blended, 30 seconds maximum. Scrape sides of bowl and beater.

Add dry mixture and water alternately, about ⅓ of each at a time, beating only until combined after each addition,

Notes:

Don't over-beat the batter at any point in preparation – you don't want to put too much air into it, or the cake will fall.

Always mix/beat on low speeds.

Variations:

Chocolate Pound Cake (page 134), French Pound Cake (page 135), Petit Fours (page 230). This is also the same recipe used for multi-tiered wedding cakes.

1–2 minutes total. Scrape down sides of bowl. The batter will be silky and thick.

Stir by hand one final time to be sure all ingredients are incorporated. Then—no matter what pan you're using—pour batter to fill the pan no more than ¾ full.

Bake until done—45 minutes for loaves or rounds, less for half-sheet pan or cupcakes. A toothpick or knife inserted in the center comes out clean; if cake is gently pressed in the middle, it bounces back to the touch.

Cool in pan on a rack until cool enough tilt out; finish cooling on rack.

THE WHISTLER

VARIATIONS: CHOCOLATE POUND CAKE

In addition to Yellow Pound Cake ingredients:
½ c cocoa powder

To convert a Yellow Pound Cake (page 132) into a Chocolate one is a total breeze. The only difference is adding ½ cup cocoa powder into the dry ingredients. That is, include it when you sift together flour, salt, baking powder, milk powder—and cocoa—then set aside.

In all other ways, just follow the Yellow Pound Cake recipe.

A BAKER'S DAUGHTER

FRENCH POUND CAKE

In addition to Yellow Pound Cake ingredients:
1 c melted chocolate fudge base (page 143)

Walnut Topping
⅛ c granulated sugar
1 c roasted walnuts, chopped

Combine sugar and walnuts in a separate bowl.

Make Yellow Pound Cake (page 132) through the step of pouring the batter into the pan(s).

Gradually heat the fudge base ("straight," no thinning)—for a few seconds at a time in the microwave, or on the stovetop—until melted and of a drizzle consistency.

For each loaf, pour half the chocolate down the length of the batter in the loaf pan.

Using a kitchen knife or thin spatula, swirl the chocolate throughout the batter in a gentle, circular pattern, down the length of the pan, being sure to dig down to the bottom of the pan to swirl all the batter.

Top with the sugar and walnut mixture. Follow baking instructions.

THE WHISTLER

ANGEL FOOD CAKE

Makes one cake in a 10" angel food cake pan, or 1 Bundt
1 c powdered sugar (measure then sift)
⅔ c cake flour (measure then sift)
13 egg whites (2 c)
¾ t salt
1 c granulated sugar
1 t vanilla extract
If desired, add about ¼ t of any other flavor extract
1½ t cream of tartar

Preheat oven to 325°F. Do NOT grease or flour the pan. However, I have learned that it helps with sticking if I cut a circle of parchment and line the bottom.

In a medium bowl, sift powdered sugar and flour together. Add half (½ cup) of the granulated sugar. Set aside.

In another bowl—either standing mixer or by hand—beat egg whites, salt, and extract(s) until just frothy, about 2–3 minutes Sprinkle cream of tartar on top; continue to beat on high (level 3) until the mixture forms stiff, glossy peaks, about 7–8 minutes. It's hard to overbeat; you want stiff peaks.

Very gently fold in remaining granulated sugar, half (¼ c) at a time, followed by the dry ingredients, in four parts.

Gently spoon batter into the pan.

Bake 38–42 minutes until golden brown, and the top springs back to the touch.

A BAKER'S DAUGHTER

Remove from the oven and turn the pan upside down to cool for 1½ hours. I find that inverting the pan over a bottle through the center cone (bracing the sides, if needed) allows the pan to remain suspended. This sets the structure of the cake and prevents both overall collapse and over-flattening of the top.

When completely cool, turn back over and carefully and completely loosen the edges (inner and outer) with a dinner knife or narrow spatula. Place a plate over the top and invert the cake, gently shaking it out onto the plate for an upside-down finish.

THE WHISTLER

YELLOW LAYER CAKE

Bring all ingredients to room temperature, except water. Grease and flour pans. Preheat oven to 325°F.

In mixing bowl—either standing mixer or by hand—sift together flour, salt, baking powder, and milk powder. Add shortening and water, beating until fluffy for no more than 1 minute.

Add vanilla, and then eggs one at a time—beating only enough to incorporate each one. After each addition, scrape sides of bowl and beater.

Add sugar; beat another 30 seconds to cream. Again scrape sides of bowl.

Stir by hand one final time to be sure all ingredients are incorporated. Then—no matter what pan you're using—pour batter to fill the pan no more than ¾ full.

Makes two 8" round layers, or one half-sheet, one Bundt, or 24 cupcakes
2¾ c cake flour
(measure then sift)
1 T salt
4 t baking powder
¼ c milk powder
1½ c shortening
1 c cold water
1½ t vanilla extract
6 eggs
2½ c granulated sugar

Notes:
Don't over-beat the batter at any point in preparation – you don't want to put too much air into it, or the cake will fall.

Always mix/beat on low speeds.

Finish with Buttercream Icing or Chocolate Fudge Icing, pages 142–143.

Bake 55–60 minutes until done—longer for Bundt pan, less for cupcakes. You'll know it's done when a toothpick or knife inserted in the center comes out clean. Also, if cake is gently pressed in the middle, it bounces back to the touch.

Cool cakes in pan on a rack until cool enough to take out; finish cooling on rack.

THE WHISTLER

VARIATION: SEVEN-LAYER CAKE

The Seven-Layer Cake is perfect for big events that require a "centerpiece" dessert. The bakery always had one on display—cut in half so that the yellow layers iced and thin layers of chocolate icing were visible. We placed the "half-circle" of cake on a cardboard half-circle and then wrapped it in plastic wrap.

By the way, the seven thin layers are formed from nearly two full cakes, with the four layers sliced horizontally (making eight thin layers) and stacked (using only seven).

Make double batches of: Yellow Layer Cake recipe on page 138. Chocolate Fudge Icing on page 142.

After all four layers of Yellow Layer Cake have cooled and set—at least a few hours, or even after refrigerating—"top" them. This means, slice the domed top off to create a flat top.

Cut all layers in half horizontally to make eight layers. For tools and tips on how to do this more easily, see Cake Techniques, page 264.

Ice and stack seven layers.

Eat the eighth layer when no one's watching. Or, even better: Share it.

A BAKER'S DAUGHTER

ICING

CHOCOLATE FUDGE ICING

If one thing made Brenner's famous, it was this icing, "*the* icing" that topped the Chocolate Top cookies—and then, with a twist, magically frosted a cake or converted into a glaze for delicate pastries.

Mix all ingredients with a standing mixer or by hand until very smooth and just turns fluffy and spreadable. Let it stand a few minutes, give it a quick mix and then check again, as it may need a bit more liquid. Add more milk or water to adjust, a little at a time.

This recipe is the way I remember it, on the bittersweet side—but you can adjust the amount of sugar to desired sweetness. If you shift sugar quantities, you might have to add a bit more liquid, too. Note: sugar also shifts the color a bit.

The icing should be moist and soft enough to pipe, but still be very fudgy and firm enough to hold the drop shape on top of the Butter Cookie. The icing will set on the outside when dry, but stay moist inside, just like Brenner's.

Variation—Fudge Pastry Glaze
For a thinner consistency—often used for Danishes, Doughnuts, Éclairs, and Brownies, but perfectly fine for cakes—it's all about the liquid. Follow the Icing recipe, gradually add about ¼ c more milk or water— as desired, for a more spreadable result. Glaze will not be stiff enough to hold a piped or spooned shape.

Chocolate Fudge Icing
Makes about a quart (32 oz., 2#)
1⅓ c chocolate fudge base (one 12-oz. container)
¾ t vanilla extract
6+ c powdered sugar (measure then sift)
¾ c+/- milk or water (don't use all at once)

About Fudge Base

If you want to make your own fudge base, there are many recipes available online. However, I get mine from a company that has been making it for more than 40 years. This base makes icing and glaze taste just like Brenner's. Tell them I sent you!

Source for Fudge Base
Party Time
3350 Bluebonnet Blvd., Baton Rouge, LA 70809
(225) 927-3270
partytimebr.com, or
contact@partytimebr.com

BUTTERCREAM ICING

This is a great all-around icing that can be used for everything—from cakes on down the line.

Beat half the shortening until fluffy. Add half the powdered sugar and blend. Add vanilla and half the water and beat until combined. Continue adding sugar and water, alternating until incorporated. Beat until light and fluffy.

The frosting should be easily spreadable. If it's too "loose" for decorating with icing, then make it stiffer by adding a bit more sugar. Store at room temperature in an air-tight container for a few days. Store longer in the refrigerator. Bring to room temperature and beat until fluffy before using.

Buttercream Icing
1⅓ c shortening
12+ c powdered sugar
(measure then sift)
4 t vanilla extract
⅔ c water or milk
(room temperature)

GELEKHTER
LAUGHTER

CHAPTER 5
MISS CHARLOTTE

My least favorite place in the entire bakery was the dark, dank basement. It was the only space for storage, and so the bakers were up and down the steep, floury, concrete steps many times a day for sacks of flour and staples. My sisters and I were mesmerized by the workings of the bakery, so we did not spend much time exploring the spooky corners downstairs. However, we did have to brave the trip when visiting the bathroom. Fortunately for my meticulous mother, there were separate bathrooms for men and women. When I peeked into the men's, there were always shoeprints and bits of paper on the floor, and smudged handprints on the door jamb. And the sink could always use a once-over.

The bakery ladies kept the women's bathroom in order—but the wall around the light switch was grayer than the paint, and that vintage infinity-loop hand towel seemed strange to me. I never knew if it just got pressed flat again, or if the machine tried to clean it somehow. It always seemed like a dingy miracle. Even so, I had the distinct impression that someone was making an effort—and that the effort was for my mother.

When she swept into the bakery, she did so lightly and with a bright grin on her face. She grabbed a wax-paper square and dipped into the sweets case, asking how the ladies were doing as she balanced a pecan sticky bun—out in the air, away from her shoes, away from her purse. She did all of this while she punched buttons on the cash register. The phrase "like she owned the

Previous page: Charlotte at the beach as a teenager. **Above:** Sweet 16 in Fairfax, Virginia, in 1948.

A BAKER'S DAUGHTER

place" was invented for Charlotte—because, strictly speaking, Max owned the place. Charlotte wasn't there very often, but when she came in, she possessed the bakery, like a visiting dignitary. The queen of baked goods.

Charlotte came to the bakery for two reasons. One was to boldly remove cash from the register. She didn't take it all, and she didn't do it daily, but when Charlotte needed cash, she just helped herself. The other reason she came was for holidays. She was a champion during those all-nighters, and she stepped in as if she'd done it all her life.

In a manner of speaking, I suppose she *had* done it all her life. My parents met when my mom's mother, Sylvia, first brought young Charlotte into the bakery on Columbia Pike. My dad was smitten from the first day. Years after her death, he wrote their "origin story" for me, just so I would have all the details. All that time later, the whole topic still made him laugh.

Your mom's mother worked at the bakery on Columbia Pike, in Arlington. Charlotte was fifteen, and she started working at the other Arlington bakery, in Westover. That's the one I worked in, and I was nineteen. It all started with us when I invited Charlotte to go on a hay ride put on by my fraternity friends from Central High School. I had graduated three years before, but they were having a sort of reunion. It was one hell of a hay ride!

We married about a year and a half later on December 5, 1949, when I was twenty-one and she was seventeen—and a senior in Falls Church High School. Before she was allowed to finish school in June, she had to sign a pledge of no discussion with other students, about her married life. Charlotte Hite was the first student to graduate, married. Of course, she would have been expelled if she became pregnant.

When I talked with Uncle Freddie about the wedding, he said he'd always thought that both fathers didn't attend the city hall wedding because they thought my parents were too young.

Dad told a different story.

We were married by a Justice of Peace, in Washington, D.C. In attendance were my mom, Charlotte's mom and her husband Gibby, and my cousin, Joe, from Seattle. My father, Louis, and her father, Charlie, refused to attend for religious objections, although neither was religious. They wrote us off as sure losers.

Later, Charlie and I became close and Pop loved Charlotte, especially after Linda was born. He would put a bag of groceries in my car every week. Never spoke about it. I don't remember ever thanking him. I hope I did. Pop would walk to our apartment, about eight blocks, just to push Linda in the baby carriage. Charlie gave us an Admiral television and we were elated, but then he gave us the payment book after putting twenty dollars down-payment. We paid fifteen dollars a month for three years, but we enjoyed that TV.

Above: Mom and Dad's wedding day, December 5, 1949.

Opposite page: Charlotte's Senior Prom 1950, Fairfax High School, Fairfax, Virginia.

When we were little, we girls weren't exactly afraid of the basement; the idea of it just made us sort of nervous and giggly. We didn't *really* think there was a goblin down there, but sometimes we would take reinforcements when we had to venture downstairs. As the youngest, I often took at least one person. Sometimes Charlotte would go with me.

Once, deep in the night on a holiday marathon, all four of us were down there—the three sisters and our mom. One sister was in the bathroom, and the other three of us were sitting on the flour sacks and stacks of newspapers, waiting our turns. It's true that we were punchy. But it's also true that Mom passed down to all of us girls her signature laugh. It's a rolling, nutty, ever-escalating giggle, and it's contagious. When we all really get tickled, we can lose ourselves to it, dissolving into puddles of hysterics, sucking everyone else into the joy of it.

So, it wasn't unusual for the bakers to hear us laughing, especially after having worked most of an all-nighter. Therefore, they ignored us in our private moment downstairs, which remained private—until now. After having three children, Mom's bladder wasn't so strong anymore, and she was trying to get whoever was in the bathroom to hurry up. We got to giggling, and then exploding with peels of our famous, crazy laughter. She couldn't help it; Mom "let loose" on a pile of newspapers, which made us all laugh even harder. It's a good thing she wasn't sitting on the flour.

MISS CHARLOTTE

Charlotte was a piece of work. And a walking contradiction. On the one hand, she presented this put-together, classy, professional persona, who was incredibly conscious of what people thought about us girls. On the other hand, once you got to know her, she was earthy and frank and a little bit shameless. She was not worried about the laughing "accident"; she found it hilarious. Her only concern was in finding a change of clothes.

Likewise, as we grew up, she "told it like it was," and she knew we were growing girls with contradictions of our own. But she was very focused on appearances. She liked to keep our less polished behaviors "in the family." She also assumed we would break rules, but was happiest when we broke them invisibly. A casual observer would have thought we were a proper bunch of ladies, and Charlotte was fine with that.

Charlotte got to be Charlotte because her father left the family when she was about six. Despite the fact that he remarried a few times—and didn't play a major role in her life after that—he hung the moon for Charlotte. She might have connected him with the ideal of a life she didn't have, because after he left, her world became so difficult. My Grandmother Sylvia—we called her Nana—was smart and savvy. She didn't cook, but she could bartend—so she ran a bar, which hosted a lot of parties. When she went to work at night, it fell to Charlotte to take care of her little brother, Alan. This part of Mom's story reminds me of sad, old movies—or sad, current reports from social services.

Above: Charlotte and her brother Alan, circa late 1930s.
Opposite page: My grandmother Sylvia "on the rocks."

A BAKER'S DAUGHTER

Because Nana was a single, working mother, a great deal of responsibility was placed on Charlotte's young shoulders. Lots of the bar folks came through Charlotte's environment, and I don't think she ever felt safe after her father left. Things got a little better in later childhood, after the bar era, when Sylvia took on another career. She assembled transistors and electronic parts with her long, nimble fingers. Decades later, I remember watching her hands. They got your attention. She talked with them, she smoked cigarettes—several packs a day—with them. I watched her mix up tuna salad or set the table for a holiday meal, which she brought in from the S&W cafeteria. Of course, I watched those hands shuffle and deal cards, count change on the table top. I see her fingers every day on my own hands. I see the shape of her face in the mirror.

Until he died, Charlotte adored her father, and also felt so abandoned by him. I'm sure it must have been confusing, being abandoned by her most favorite person in the world. I could always sense the yearning she had for him. Later, in her last days, when Mom was dying of cancer, she said her father was "out in the hall smoking a cigarette, waiting."

Charlotte turned out to be a beautiful Southern woman with a great sense of style. You could hear her Southernness in the slant of her speech, in her vowels, rounded and slow. You could see her Southernness in the hats she wore, and in her finishing-school walk—whether she was wearing spike heels or tennis shoes.

MISS CHARLOTTE

She learned to walk with a book on her head, upright but not stiff, her body swaying and bending like a weeping willow tree. She never left the house without perfect makeup and a coordinated outfit. And the house looked just as put together. I can see her making everything match in heaven right at this moment.

Even considering this elegance, there was nothing she couldn't or wouldn't do; there was nothing that Charlotte avoided. When difficult things happened, she never flinched: "You have to go down the middle of things, there's no getting around them," she would say. And, during the doldrums: "If you're feeling down, put on some lipstick and you'll feel better."

These were the things she had to give. You shared your heart with Max, and you learned the ropes from Charlotte. She wasn't a nurturer; she was that older girl in college who always had an extra tampon in her purse. My mom went back to work the second I was eligible for nursery school—where they served juice with hard, iced, oatmeal cookies. Charlotte had stayed at home with all of us, but as soon as she could "do something," she did. It was all about not sitting still.

She first went to work in her father's Merchant Van Lines office, and then—fortunately and unfortunately—in the administrative office of the high school I eventually attended. For the students there, she was fun; she sewed on buttons, handed out advice, stashed changes of clothes under her desk for an endless array of teenaged emergencies. When the kids weren't hers, she could be a confidante, a shoulder, the coolest adult they knew. Most of all, she was the keeper of the hall passes. Everyone who knew how to make her laugh could get a coveted escape from class. This came in handy for my friends and me, since we could be very persuasive about how awful the school lunches were. If we remained punctual, she was good for a trip to McDonald's or Pizza Hut. If Mr. Skinner, the truant officer, appeared when we were about to make a run for it, he honored our informal don't-ask-don't-tell arrangement. Before stepping into prohibited territory, we would hover—with the toes of our shoes overhanging the sidewalk edge—until his tail lights disappeared around the corner. Like everyone on campus, he loved my mom—so when he saw my gaggle of friends, he just laughed and kept moving.

Of course, having my mom in my environment all day also clipped my wings. She couldn't show me too much privilege—so I had to develop especially good strategies to get around her. I also was made an example of by the teachers at school. When I "forgot" to erase the trig formulas off my hand, or smoked in the bathroom, I received a harsher sentence than anyone else—and Mom learned about it, when any other parent wouldn't have.

In our family life, Dad had a similar reality. She was always watching, even if it was from afar. Charlotte created an orderly life that he would not have created for himself, and she raised his standards. She set up his family life, his closet, his schedule outside of work. But somehow, he didn't lose himself in the process.

MISS CHARLOTTE

And as powerful as she was, she didn't try to overpower him. If anyone except her father might have hung the moon, it was Max.

A few years before she died, when my mom and I had talked about my parents' early life, she said, "Your father and I used to neck on the bank of the Potomac River. We had always dreamed of living on the river someday." Her eyes had turned all faraway and dreamy.

The house they ultimately built when I was a teenager was beautiful—and it was on that river. It was on the fancier side of nice, with brick and wrought iron and fireplaces. They got to live their dreams in so many ways, but in terms of homes, I watched them do it. Well, some of it. They bought their first house in about 1951, a house they could "afford, but it pinched" in Pimmit Hills. When that mortgage became more comfortable, they bought up to the next afford-but-it-pinched house, in Brookland. They were patient and enjoyed where they lived at each stage of the journey, but kept moving toward their goal. It's an example that served me well—because I learned how to be patient, too. I also got to live in the river house. I was thirteen, and Stevie Wonder's *Songs in the Key of Life* had just been released. Dad and I played it on our new stereo system until the grooves were gone.

The filthy, poor conditions of Charlotte's childhood home created a frenzied fastidiousness that was impossible to satisfy throughout her life. She never wanted to live like that again—and as long as she was in control of her life, it was going to be spotless and organized. It was also going to be fun, yet civilized. Her compulsions sometimes made it difficult to be her daughter, but her love was undeniable. I learned to rely on her fierceness. I relied on it to teach me everything that is useful in life every day: cooking, sewing, how to balance a checkbook, run a house, throw a party, and write a thank you note. Charlotte—thanks to her own survival—encouraged me to learn typing, shorthand, and, later, computers, so I could always get a job. She taught us to be as uncompromisingly independent as she had been; she made sure I had $5 in my wallet in case I needed to get home from a date. She did not allow any of her girls to rely on anyone else, especially a man. For us, Charlotte represented what was absolutely female. She tended to our womanhood.

This kind of attention and fondness, this kind of enduring love, is something my family assumed. It was what I loved most about my parents as a couple. Charlotte loved my dad, and Max loved her. Of course, they had their share of marital struggles, but even still, if I came home early from school, I might find them skinny-dipping in the pool. Their love centered my life. They talked about their dreams, dreams they made together, and I could see these dreams in their eyes. Their way together sparked dreams of my own.

Dad's eyes would shine when he talked about Mom. I know what he loved about her, I saw him grab her "tuchus" and tease her about her overbite, which he adored. He told me he loved

Charlotte strutting her stuff. I've always wondered if this was taken by one of her boyfriends, pre-Max.

Loretta Lynn because she "has buck teeth just like your mama." Eventually, Max would change the lyrics to Johnny Mercer's old tune, "Ugly Chile" to accommodate Charlotte's buck teeth.

This is how it actually goes:

Hey! You're ugly, oh! so ugly
You're some ugly chile…
You're knock kneed, pigeon toed, box ankled
You're big foot, barefoot, slue footed too

I can still hear Dad's lilt: "She had buck teeth, knock knees, and pigeon toes, she was an *ugly chile*.…" It was funny only because she was *not* an ugly chile.

"Charlotte, you would have to have a complete facial reconstruction if you had that beautiful overbite corrected!" he'd tease her. "You couldn't eat corn on the cob so well, and what would you do if you could put your lips together?" When she'd fall asleep in the passenger seat on the long drive to the beach, Dad would wait until she "fell out," before he'd say, "I hope a bee doesn't fly into her mouth!" Mom would wake up enough to slap him playfully.

We also knew exactly what Mom loved in Dad. "Your father can't wiggle his hips," she'd say after their ballroom dance class—one of their special indulgences. "I try to show him. I take him by his little butt but it's no use. He can do the steps, though!"

A BAKER'S DAUGHTER

she'd beam across the kitchen. They danced together often, both in the house and out at bars and parties.

And being a family that talked about money, sex, and death, we knew what drove them crazy in a not-so-good way, too. I would have to warn my friends about the candor in our family. Our truth-telling, wacky sense of humor, finding the raw funny in things that other families didn't even talk about. For her grown-up friends, it was easy be around Charlotte. She was attentive, energetic, and fun. She had a multitude of loving, loyal and fun-loving compatriots. Both my parents did. They were funny as hell.

From the outside, she seemed to effortlessly manage our home. As it turned out, she put everything she had into it. It would take me decades to fully understand the subtler dynamics of my parents' married life—and how close we once were to my mom's walking away. Or, more accurately, how close I came to not existing at all.

My parents were gamers—the old-fashioned kind, before "gaming" meant computer games. Dad enjoyed cards, and Mom loved board games, cards, and socializing—just like Nana Sylvia had when Mom was little. Dad's family, it turned out, was no different. Here's how he described it:

> *My Dad and his brothers all liked to gamble—horse racing, poker, dice, pinochle, rummy of all types, and a daily numbers game. My mother and all us children liked to gamble, also. Mom once hit the number*

666 for five cents and received $27.00. She was so elated that when the number writer asked if she wanted to play a number the next day, she said, "Yes, play 666 again for a nickel." Against big odds, she hit again and got $27.00 more. Pop could not get over her just playing like that, for so little money. Because he played for higher stakes, he told her he would be rich if he hit two days in a row. This happened in about 1936, in Southwest Washington, D.C. Mom went out and bought herself a new dress and something for all of us. Remember, we were a family of nine children and two parents. Everyone in Southwest heard about the great luck, and they came around looking for a handout, but she had spent all the winnings. I think she knew they would be around.

Pop took me to the movies one Saturday, and we walked from 4th Street in Southwest D.C. to 9th Street in Northwest, D.C. After the movie, we ate in a roast beef restaurant, Hodges, where they served a sandwich for ten cents, including all the pickles you wanted. After eating, Pop took me to the Bakers Union Hall, where he proceeded to play poker. I watched for a while and it was really exciting to hear those guys argue and cuss all the time. They started giving me five cents from each pot, and my pockets were getting full. I finally fell asleep on a bench, and when Pop was out of money he and I walked home. It was morning by then. I had fallen asleep thinking how I was going to spend all that money—but when I awoke all the nickels were gone. Pop had needed the money. My dream of a windfall went bye-bye, but I never regretted losing the coins. It was a great experience.

My earliest memories are of the grownups—my parents and a few friends, or sometimes our extended family—playing poker at our dining room table. That same table is down in my dining room right now. My parents had a big plastic bowl of change they used for poker nights. It was from this bowl that Dad taught me about money. I was the youngest, and the most indulged, but I also had fevers as a young child. My ear infections gave me license to slip down to the kitchen dripping with sweat, not sure if I was hallucinating or really hearing laughter. I still can smell the Old Granddad bourbon, the cigarette smoke. I can still see the adults being adults. I loved slipping into their world. I would be all hot and floppy, half unconscious, willing to be transported on their magic carpet to oblivion.

Our whole family also played games together—and even went to the racetrack with Dad, or with Nana Sylvia and her entourage. My mother's mother never changed. She traveled through middle age and beyond, in the next phase of her "bar era." She spent each and every day at the track with her husband, Gibby—and her ex, my granddad Charlie. They stayed dear friends for their entire lives. Nana Sylvia was my first example of a divorced woman, and she broke any mold I ever imagined about women and grandmothers. If the emphysema hadn't killed her lungs, she might still be alive. The rest of her was invincible.

I loved the energy of the racetrack. It was like a circus crossed with a baseball game. I'd get a hot dog and ice cream, all the

while attempting to make out the announcer's crackly voice over the loud speaker. I loved all the lingo—exacta, daily double, win, place, show. Across the board. We sat in the bleachers under a corrugated roof, and I'd peer down at the beautiful horses walking around, coming off the track. Dad would let me pick one to bet on. I'd go by the name. I'd make my bet and get my ticket, hold it safe. I would root for my horse and squint to see it run. I pretended that every one of my picks was Secretariat. Dad had binoculars, but they were hard for me to use. I liked to hold them, though, because it made me feel like a grown-up, and like I was really there with him, that we were doing something together. It was a thrill to win money, but the biggest thrill was just to hang out with Dad.

He didn't really have another indulgence that I knew of. He would sometimes fish, and he was good on the water. When I was in junior high and high school, he'd pull my friends and me behind the boat on our water skis. I saw him as the quintessential worker, the responsible yet mellow dad, and a typical east-coast beach and river guy.

Much later, I learned that my dad had some darkness deep within him. His gambling was more than a social pastime. It came bundled with a compulsion that got legs when he was a young man. He drank some when he gambled, too, but mostly he smoked. He enjoyed the paraphernalia of it—the pack, the cigarette, the lighter, the ash tray.

When I heard about all of this, I interpreted the gambling indulgence as an addiction, or perhaps a more mild, silent protest against working all hours. All day. Every day. It turns out that he came by all of this honestly. All of the Brenners loved to gamble; Dad's youngest brother—Fred, the only non-baking brother—was a professional gambler.

When I finally heard and truly understood the larger story about my dad, I realized that he needed Charlotte. I had always thought that she was lucky to have him—that anyone who ever knew him was lucky to have him. Until I knew about his demons, I thought he was kind of doing her a favor to fall in love with her. She wasn't always likable.

But in the end, she saved him. She saved us all.

When I started to understand that Max wasn't "all Superman, all the time," I remembered Charlotte's mantra: you have to go down the middle of things. So I gathered my courage and put one foot in front of the other.

I walked straight down the center line, toward whatever the truth was:

Before I was born, when my sisters were toddlers, the cards took Max away from his young bride and daughters. He'd smoke and drink, and gamble away money they didn't have. Mom's straight back and carefully ordered life brought him around, time and again—and like the tide he would come back in, agree to back off of the table. And then he would get caught in the rip.

Charlotte's locket, which for my whole life carried this photo of Max—at the racetrack.

The perfect storm came when he made a different kind of gamble—and started his own small doughnut shop, the ultimate test of the Brenner lineage. Just as he was finding his footing as an independent baker, he lost the shop. It wasn't because of the gambling—the shop just failed—but Max hit bottom. His whole life was staring back at him. Black-and-white Christmas snapshots from that year reveal our family's meager surroundings—the only furniture in the living room was lawn furniture, the kind with colored plastic straps that weave between aluminum frames to form the seat.

Charlotte put the hammer down. She had known poverty and instability, and she was not interested in knowing them again. She told him, one last time, about the rules of engagement if he wanted to keep the buck-toothed, knock-kneed beauty in his life. She was ready to roll. She didn't want to, but she was ready.

He tamed the beast—not Charlotte, but the gambling. He focused on picking up the pieces of his business life and went back to "home base." He rejoined his dad and his brother Willie and started again, this time at the Alexandria bakery. There, he found a rhythm that could include daughters and customers and cakes and doughnuts and fishing—and one very intense overbite. He grew up. His life was coming back together.

She proved she was all-in by becaming pregnant with me, the third daughter, eight years younger than the sister before.

Charlotte gave him one more chance. And he took it.

A BAKER'S DAUGHTER

SOUL FOOD

When it came to food, our home kitchen was not our lifeblood. The bakery was, and we all associated sustenance with Dad. Mom did fix dinner each night, but food simply was not her thing. She had tired of survival-living by the time she was ten—so she loved restaurant food. Fried soft-shell crab sandwiches and Crab Imperial. She put mayonnaise in and on everything, and then looked to Max for "something sweet" after a meal.

We didn't always have something from the bakery, so Dad—after working all day—would finish his plate and quietly shuffle into the kitchen. We'd hear the clatter of pans, stirring, bowls ringing on the counter. Within minutes, he'd appear with a glorious, rich custard—the one with no recipe card, which I tried to replicate in this book—or something else equally amazing. As far as I could tell, he made these things "from nothing."

Although the bakery wasn't Charlotte's "place," she did make an indelible impact there. She was the one who devised the brilliant system for handling the barrage of holiday orders. She organized the hundreds of preorders, impaled the filled tickets on the metal skewer, arranged the box-assembly process, and made sure there were plenty of plastic bags and spools of string. She created a pickup and logging stations, to be sure that we correctly matched each order with its number and its customer.

Of the precise selection of tasks my mother performed at the bakery, there was only one she did poorly. When making sales,

she needed to use her fingers to double-check her math—before turning around to count back a customer's change. As smart as she was, her brain froze in this process.

What Mom loved best in the bakery—besides my dad—was the right side of the front display cases. That's where her favorite pecan sticky buns were—but she also scooted open the white sliding doors to snatch a doughnut. Maybe just a simple glazed, maybe a cream-filled. For just a bite, she would choose a doughnut hole. When the bakers were frying doughnuts, people could smell them all throughout the shopping center. Mom always tried to talk Dad into reorienting the vent system so that it would blow the aroma out into the parking lot. He smiled at her, but he never did it.

On a special day, she would wander to the left side, to the tall display cases. She usually went for the first one, which was refrigerated. Beyond its frosty moisture in the corners of the glass were chocolate éclairs, cream puffs, Black Forest cake, lemon meringue, and chocolate cream pie. The recipes in this chapter are hers, and they all are her Southern favorites.

At the end of my mother's life, she wondered aloud about what she ever did to receive so much love in her life. She didn't see herself as special; she didn't expect anything. She personified the Southern women's rule: keep your expectations low. But she added another rule: make your own rules. She did think there were ways to do things, and she did them, but she made no suppositions about what anyone else was to do. Except for Max. And us girls.

During those last days, we sat together in the room she shared with dad, rocking back and forth in a deep, dark, spiritual reckoning. I wanted to help her through, help her find some peace—and like an answer to a prayer, I remembered a box in her closet. It was overflowing with those little school pictures of caps and gowns, with words of love on the back written to her from hundreds of students.

She had carried this box with her when she and Max had retired to North Carolina. And then she had forgotten about it. One at a time, I showed her a picture and read the words on the back. There were letters, too. It was a box of evidence that she had done a good thing—connected with young people. Those kids looked forward to making her laugh; they loved her. They also knew she loved them.

As we looked through her past that day—as she witnessed herself through the eyes of hundreds of kids who did not live in her house, or follow her rules—she allowed herself to receive their love. She relaxed a little, starting to believe she had done something worthwhile in her life. In truth, her plain talk and "going down the middle of things" had saved many kids; several had even stayed in our home for a spell.

This box provided the safer route that day, safer than talking about us. And it worked just fine. In the end, the love she was really talking about—the love she craved—was my dad's. When it got close to the end for her, she wanted to just be alone with him.

Still, it was my honor to help care for my mom as she passed through the stages of the illness that would take her life. One day, we left on an unexpected high note—one that got us to giggling. She had recalled volunteering to chaperone the boys' varsity basketball team on the bus to an away game, just as rap music had become a thing. "I wanted to sit in the back with those boys to make sure they didn't get into mischief," she told me, her face breaking into delighted memory. Even with her illness, the irrepressible giggle started to rise in her chest, and I couldn't help but to join her. "One boy started by rhythmically saying, 'somebody-give-me-the-beat, somebody-give-me-the-beat,' and then others started making beat sounds with their mouths and hands. Then one of the boys started reciting poetry to the beat—they really did, and it was good," said my white Protestant Southern mama. "It was great, we had so much fun!"

As I bake an éclair or pour filling into a pecan pie, I think about small moments like this. I remember her teaching me to like coconut cream pie—I remember my first-ever bite of it—or talking about something silly a girlfriend said. I see her pinch my dad, and I hear her laugh.

I love that I can still hear her laugh.

VANILLA CUSTARD

After I grew out of the yellow-cake-with-white-icing-and-pink-ballerinas-on-top birthday-cake phase, I often asked Dad to decorate a Boston Cream Pie for my birthday cake. When researching this book, I learned that the bakery used a purchased cream mix for their custard, so there was no ingredient list for this recipe. However, since Chocolate Eclairs, custard-filled Doughnuts—and, of course, Boston Cream Pie—are some of my top favorites, I worked this one out.

For the record, ballerinas look great on a Boston Cream Pie.

Makes 4+ cups, one medium saucepan full
6 egg yolks
6 c whole milk
(or half-and-half)
1 c granulated sugar
⅔ c cornstarch
½ t salt
1 T vanilla extract

In a medium bowl or glass measuring cup, beat eggs, then gradually stir in the milk (or half-and-half) until blended.

Prepare a large pan (one large enough to accommodate the saucepan below) with ice water; set aside.

Mix sugar, cornstarch, and salt in a large, heavy saucepan. Gradually stir in a small amount of the liquid mixture, enough to make a smooth paste. Be sure to incorporate all of the dry mixture. Slowly stir in the remaining liquid mixture until blended.

Cook custard over medium-low heat, stirring constantly. Be sure to stir all the way around the bottom and sides, and continue until

Variation
Quick Vanilla Custard Filling—Max's home shortcut

Dad used to create a quick custard by "doctoring" a vanilla pudding mix. He would follow the pie filling instructions with the following tweaks: Instead of milk, use half and half (or at least whole milk) so it will be thicker. After pudding thickens, take off the heat and add 1 t of vanilla and 1 T of butter. Let it cool completely if using for filling. Note: this is an easy custard, but it does not have the texture and flavor of the scratch recipe. I would not recommend this for Boston Cream Pie or Éclairs, as it is too thin.

the mixture thickens and comes to a boil (about 25–30 minutes). Be patient here! You're getting close when large bubbles appear and the spoon drags in the thickening custard. Let it boil for one more minute and immediately remove from heat.

Cool quickly in the pan of ice water, very gently stirring only occasionally until well-cooled. Vigorous stirring will make it thin.

Stir in vanilla until blended.

Press a piece of plastic wrap onto the surface of the custard to prevent a skin from forming. Refrigerate until completely chilled—for at least an hour, but four hours are better, and overnight is great.

Now it's ready to use for filling. Never use warm filling, as it will make an Éclair soggy. Everyone hates a soggy Éclair.

MISS CHARLOTTE

PIE CRUST

All-around pie crust; always reliable, flaky, delicious.

Makes two 9" pie crusts
3¼ c cake flour
(or all-purpose)
¼ c granulated sugar
1 T salt
2 c shortening
(refrigerator cold)
½–¾ c water (ice cold)

In a mixing bowl—either standing mixer or by hand—combine flour, sugar and salt.

Add shortening using a pastry cutter, two table knives, or dough hook attachment until the mixture is in pea-sized chunks.

While mixing, add ½ c of the cold water to the dry mixture until combined. (Add additional water or flour if needed, 1 T at a time—but allow dough to be on the rather moist side.) Gently finish the dough on an abundantly floured surface with well-floured hands to combine into a smooth dough. Don't over work it. Stop when it's combined and just smooth, a wonderfully delicate dough.

Cut the dough in half, roll each half into a smooth ball.

Place one dough ball on an abundantly floured surface, dust the top of the dough ball with flour and roll (or press) to about ¼" thick, using well-floured hands and/or rolling pin.

Allow the dough to roll onto the rolling pin, or your hand/forearm. You may need to use a scraper in this process, as the dough is fragile and might stick to your surface and break if it isn't floured enough.

Carefully lift and unroll dough into the pie pan. Gently move the dough to the center of the pan, allowing dough to drape over the edge. If the dough breaks, you can gently press it back together or roll it out again (but it won't be quite as flaky the more you work it.) Cut the excess dough from beyond the edge of the pan, then pinch or cut the crust, finishing the edge.

Either fill or bake the crusts, depending on your recipe.

For a filled pie, you can make your own pie filling or use a prepared pie filling. Two cans of your favorite are enough. This recipe makes enough dough for two single-crust pies or one double-crust pie. The second crust can be used whole—vented with holes to let air escape—or cut. Cut tops can be woven into a lattice pattern, or placed as cutouts.

If filled, bake at 350°F until light brown, with darker edges and the filling is bubbling, about 40–45 minutes. Unfilled, poke some holes in the bottom with a fork to let air escape, and bake for 5 minutes or until brown.

MISS CHARLOTTE

PUMPKIN PIE

All you need to know about this Pumpkin Pie is that it won the "Best Pumpkin Pie in the Washington Metro Area" award. Year after year.

Makes two 9" pies
⅛ c cornstarch
1 t salt
1 t cinnamon
⅛ t ginger
⅛ t cloves
4¾ c canned pumpkin
⅓ c honey
¼ c vegetable oil
1½ granulated sugar
2½ c evaporated milk
4 eggs (lightly beaten with fork)
2 pie crusts (unbaked)

Preheat oven to 425°F.

In a small bowl, whisk together cornstarch, salt, cinnamon, ginger, and cloves.

In large bowl—either standing mixer or by hand—combine pumpkin, honey, and oil.

Add sugar and mix until combined. Add evaporated milk and mix until combined.

Add dry ingredients, mixing until combined and smooth.

Add eggs all at once; mix until combined.

A BAKER'S DAUGHTER

Pour half the mixture into each crust, not filling beyond the bottom of the crimped edge.

Use foil or a pie crust ring so the edge it won't over brown.

Bake 15 minutes at 425°F, then 43–47 minutes at 325, until a toothpick inserted into the center of the pie comes out clean.

MISS CHARLOTTE

PECAN PIE

Makes two 9" pies
4 c corn syrup (Karo)
⅔ c brown sugar
1 t salt
1½ t vanilla extract
⅛ c cake flour
(or all-purpose)
⅓ c shortening
6 eggs (lightly beaten)
1 c whole pecans
1 c chopped pecans
(chop, then measure)
2 pie crusts (unbaked)

Roast Chopped Pecans at 350°F until they are browned and smell roasted. Leave the oven on.

In a large sauce pan, stir together syrup, sugar, salt, and vanilla.

Add flour and shortening. Heat on low to medium until the butter melts.

When the mixture cools to the touch (it will start to thicken), add the eggs and stir until well combined and smooth.

Stir in all of the chopped pecans until combined.

A BAKER'S DAUGHTER

Pour half the mixture into each crust, not filling beyond the bottom of the crimped edge. Top with whole pecans.

Line oven rack with a piece of foil and bake for 55–60 minutes at 350°F. This is a long bake time—at 30 minutes, cover the edges with foil or a pie crust shield to avoid their over baking. However, check and remove before end of bake time if the edges needs more browning.

When done, the top will be puffed up and set, and the center should not wobble when you jiggle the pie. Allow to cool completely before slicing.

MISS CHARLOTTE

COCONUT CUSTARD PIE

Charlotte taught me how to love coconut. We would eat this pie right out of the pan. And then we'd go for the macaroons.

Makes two 9" pies
1 c granulated sugar
½ c milk powder
¼ c cornstarch
¼ c shortening
4 eggs
4 c water (room temp)
1 t vanilla extract
pinch salt
pinch ground nutmeg
2 c shredded coconut (sweetened)
Two pie crusts (unbaked)

Whisk together sugar, milk powder, cornstarch in a mixing bowl.

Melt shortening in a medium sauce pan; turn off heat. Add sugar mixture and stir until combined.

Add eggs, one at a time, stirring for 30 seconds after each. Add water, vanilla, salt, and nutmeg; mix until combined.

Heat on medium for 15–30 minutes until thickened, stirring constantly, don't allow mixture to boil or thicken too fast.

Preheat oven to 400°F.

Pour half the batter into each pie crust, not filling beyond the bottom of crimped edge.

Sprinkle half of the coconut over each filled pie. Encourage some of the coconut to sink by gently patting with the spoon. Some of the coconut should stay up on top.

Bake 55–65 minutes until set. Be sure to bake until the top and edges are deep golden brown, or crust will be soggy. If needed, cover edges loosely with a piece of foil or a pie crust shield to avoid their over baking. However, check and remove before end of bake time if the edges needs more browning.

MISS CHARLOTTE

COCONUT MACAROONS

Okay, it's possible that these were Mom's favorite.

Makes about 2 dozen
2⅓ c powdered sugar
2½ T all-purpose flour
2 t salt
2 t vanilla extract
3–4 egg whites
(3 if large, 4 if medium)
4 c shredded coconut
(if sweetened, reduce sugar to 2 cups)

Preheat oven to 350°F.

Combine all the ingredients in a bowl and mix together. This dough needs to be rather wet—but dry enough to hold together. Start with three egg whites, and then add the fourth if needed.

Heat through on the stovetop, stirring often, on low before sheeting.

Spoon or scoop drops of about 2T onto a parchment-lined or well-greased baking sheet, 1" apart. Use two spoons to scoop and the back of the spoons to shape dough into a pointed mound.

Bake for 16–17 minutes, turning the baking sheet in the middle of the bake, until the peaks of coconut are deep golden brown.

Allow to almost fully cool on the baking sheet before peeling off.

Variations:
You can add flavoring like almond (about ¼ t) to the macaroons—either instead, of or along with, the vanilla.

I like to drizzle or dip in about ½ cup melted semi-sweet chocolate chips.

MISS CHARLOTTE

DANISH PASTRY

Dad's best friend was Tom Harris. Every year, Dad and Tom would go fishing on the James River. Dad would bring Tom's favorite, cherry Danish pastry.

"One year, we were in the canoe fishing, and Tom put his fishing rod down to eat his Danish. He always ate it from the outside in, peeling off the rounds of pastry. This time, he finally got to the end, and had that cherry center in his fingers—when he dropped it in the water!" Dad said, cracking up. "The look on his face, the poor guy, like his dog just died!"

Makes about 2 dozen medium (about 4" round) pastries
2 T active dry yeast
5¾ c all-purpose flour
⅔ c granulated sugar
⅓ c milk powder
1 T salt
1 c water (105–110°F)
⅔ c margarine (or salted butter)
1 egg
1 t vanilla extract
1 t lemon juice
1½ c (3 sticks) margarine, cold (or salted butter)

STAGE 1 PREPARATION
Prepare two parchment-lined baking sheets.

In a large mixing bowl—either standing mixer or by hand—whisk together yeast, flour, sugar, milk powder, and salt.

Prepare warm water, add ⅔ c margarine/butter, egg, vanilla, and lemon juice. Gently bring mixture back up to 105–110°F, using either the microwave oven or stovetop.

Slowly add warm water mixture to the dry mixture while stirring by hand or on level 1 with standing mixer. Scrape sides and hook.

Note:
Dough can be made ahead and stored in the refrigerator. Just warm at room temperature for about 30 minutes. Then roll, cut, shape, proof, fill and bake.

At this point, dough should be on the sticky side. If needed, add a few more tablespoons of water to give it enough moisture to come together—but without making it too sticky; if it's already too sticky, add a bit of flour.

Mix at level 1 or by hand for about 3–5 minutes, until dough is smooth and elastic—just past sticky. Don't use a higher setting, as you don't want to incorporate a bunch of air.

Press/pat into a square shape and loosely wrap with plastic. Place in the refrigerator for 20–30 minutes.

MISS CHARLOTTE

STAGE 2 PREPARATION

Prepare the second measure of margarine/butter by cutting all three sticks lengthwise in half, to make 6 equal pieces. Lay 3 of them on plastic wrap to make a rectangle. Cover with another piece of plastic wrap. Pound and roll with a rolling pin to make a rectangle of margarine/butter, about 6" x 9". Put it in the fridge (or briefly in freezer) to chill. Repeat with the other 3 pieces. You'll have two rectangles, each made with 1½ sticks.

Place half the dough on a well-floured surface or board; put other half back in refrigerator. With a well-floured rolling pin, roll into a rectangle about 10" x 16", being sure to keep flour on the surface under the dough. Gently pat the air bubbles out, as needed.

Place half of one of the chilled butter pieces in the middle of the rectangle, fold dough over left and right to make a rectangle package. Keep the margarine/butter within 1–2" from the edge of the dough. Turn ¼ and roll back out to the large rectangle size. Place the other half of the butter, fold left and right to make a dough package. Press/pinch the ends and the folded edge together to form a closed dough package.

Do the same for the other half of the dough and margarine/butter. Place both back in the refrigerator for 30 minutes.

A BAKER'S DAUGHTER

FINISHING

For each package/half, repeat and fold as above (but without adding butter!): roll out to 10" x 16", fold twice; roll again and fold twice—four folds in total, per half. Place back in refrigerator for at least 2 hours, but overnight is better.

Take one dough package at a time out of the fridge and roll out to a 12" x 18" rectangle. Make several ½" lengthwise cuts with a pizza cutter or pastry knife to make strips of dough. This should result in about 12 strips.

Working with one strip at a time, place it in its spot on the baking sheet, as they're challenging to move once shaped. Roll from the center out to make a long rope of dough. Keep flouring hands and surface well. Shape the dough into a flat spiral, and tuck the loose end under. You can twist the rope to create a nice look.

Do the same with the rest of the strips.

Previous page:
Marcy making Danish Pastry with young helper Adelaide Winful, in Marcy's kitchen.

A BAKER'S DAUGHTER

Chocolate Pastry Glaze
Makes about a quart
(32 oz., 2#)
1 ⅓ c chocolate fudge base (one 12-oz. container; see page 258)
¾ t vanilla extract
6+ c powdered sugar (measure then sift)
1 c milk or water (don't use all at once)

Mix ingredients until very smooth and fluffy. Let stand a few minutes; check consistency; adjust liquid as needed. Will not be stiff enough to hold a piped or spooned shape.

Powdered Sugar Drizzle/Icing
6+ c powdered sugar (measure then sift)
⅓+ c milk or water (a little at a time)
⅛ c (2 T) vanilla extract

Mix ingredients. To achieve a pourable consistency, you might need a bit more liquid.

PROOFING & FILLING

Let rise at room temperature for about 30–90 minutes, until puffy. The Dimple Test (page 271) will let you know when it's done.

Near the end of the rising time, preheat oven to 400°F.

Fill pastries with a tablespoon of filling, pressing down into the middle of the pastry with your spoon.

This is a sweet Danish, so premade pie fillings work great: apple, cherry, blueberry, or cheese (ricotta/cream cheese/sugar/egg). You can also use marzipan almond paste, melted chocolate, Chocolate Pastry Glaze, preserves, or jams.

BAKING & GARNISHING

Just before putting in the oven, brush the dough spiral with Egg Wash (page 276). Bake 16–18 minutes, until deep golden brown.

After cool, you can add Powdered Sugar Drizzle/Icing, if desired. Or maybe garnish with nuts.

MISS CHARLOTTE

DOUGHNUTS

I never met a doughnut I didn't like. Ever. This might be because of my privileged childhood, in which I was able to eat them straight off the glazing pan. Nothing in this world is as good as a freshly glazed doughnut, or a raspberry-filled just off the filler. All of that goodness happened on the work table next to the stainless doughnut fryer and hood vent. The doughnut filler was metal and shaped like an anvil—and just as heavy—with a metal handle. A cooked doughnut would be impaled on the tip and when the handle was depressed, a perfect dose of jelly or cream filled the doughnut.

Unfortunately, the only Brenner's list of ingredients I have for doughnuts is for a plain doughnut—a regular, yeast, raised doughnut. But still: this recipe is the base for many other things, including Pecan Loaf, Sticky Buns, and Apple Cinnamon Nut Loaf. So we're safe there. Brenner's doughnuts shall live on.

In a story unrelated to deliciousness, I often imagined the surprise of an actual hoodlum who once broke into the bakery through the doughnut-fryer vent hood. His or her mission, evidently, was not to steal anything, but just to commit some criminal mischief. It had to be a bummer when two feet landed in the vat of grease.

A BAKER'S DAUGHTER

Makes about 2 dozen

1 T active dry yeast
1½ t salt
¼ c sugar
2 t baking powder
⅛ c milk powder
4¼ c all-purpose flour
(or 1¾ c cake flour +
2½ c bread flour)
1⅛ c water
(105–110°F)
⅓ c shortening
2 eggs
1 t vanilla extract
1 t lemon juice

STAGE 1 PREPARATION

Prepare proof bowl and proof spot. (For details on how, see Bread Notes page 269.)

In a mixing bowl—either standing mixer or by hand—combine yeast, salt, sugar, baking powder, milk powder, and flour.

Pour 1⅛ hot tap water (typically 105–110°F) into a 2-cup glass measuring cup. Drop in shortening to melt. Add eggs, vanilla, and lemon juice to water/shortening mixture. Mix well, beating lightly with a fork.

Gently bring this liquid mixture back to 105–110°F. If you need to warm it, do so gradually in microwave or on the stovetop.

MISS CHARLOTTE

Slowly add the warm liquid mixture to the dry mixture on setting 1 in standing mixer with dough hook, or by hand for a minute or less. Using setting 2, knead for about 3–5 minutes (about 7 minutes by hand) until smooth and silky. The dough will pull away from the dough hook when you lift it. This dough is sticky, so resist the urge to add flour. If kneading by hand, you'll need to use the scraper/hand method (see Bread Notes page 269).

Gently turn out and scrape into the prepared bowl. Turn the dough over so the top is oiled. This keeps it moist so it won't crack and rising will be smooth.

Cover with plastic and place in your warm proof spot (70–90°F) until puffy and almost doubled in size. This usually takes about 1–2 hours, but timing will depend on many factors. It's best to just watch what the dough is doing, rather than relying on the clock. Check every 20 minutes.

STAGE 2 PREPARATION

When dough has almost (but not quite) doubled in size, gently tilt it onto your lightly floured board or counter surface. Flour your hands. Sprinkle the dough with a little bit of flour.

Cut dough in half. For each half, fold and shape into a smooth ball. Cover with floured plastic and let rest for 10 minutes.

Roll dough out to $1/4$–$1/2$" thick.

Using a doughnut cutter, cut out doughnuts; place on a parchment-lined or greased baking sheet. Allow to rise until puffy, but not double in size, using the Dimple Test (page 271) to confirm when it's done.

Variations:

Cinnamon Swirls
(Shown at right.)
Roll out half the dough to about ¼–½" thick. Generously coat with a layer of cinnamon. Roll the dough into a log. Cut ½" rounds, place on parchment-lined or greased baking sheet. Do the same with the other half. Continue with the final proof, frying, cooling, and glazing/topping instructions.

Braided Doughnut
Roll out three logs of dough about ¼–½" thick. Braid the full length, then cut to the sizes you want. Continue with the final proof, frying, cooling, and glazing/topping instructions.

MISS CHARLOTTE

FRYING

In a frying or cast-iron pan with high sides, or a stand-alone fryer, start to heat about 4" of vegetable oil (the doughnuts need to float) to 350–375°F.

You're going to work with only as many doughnuts as can fit in your pot without crowding. Place all remaining uncooked doughnuts in the refrigerator to slow down their rise while frying the others. Then gently place selected doughnuts into the hot oil. Fry until light brown; turn over. When both sides are brown, remove from the oil and drain on paper towels.

Powdered Sugar Drizzle/Icing

6+ c powdered sugar (measure then sift)
⅓ + c milk or water (a little at a time)
⅛ c (2 T) vanilla extract

Mix ingredients. To achieve a pourable consistency, you might need a bit more liquid.

Chocolate Pastry Glaze

Makes about a quart (32 oz., 2#)
1⅓ c chocolate fudge base (one 12-oz. container; see page 258)
¾ t vanilla extract
6+ c powdered sugar (measure then sift)
1 c milk or water (don't use all at once)

Mix ingredients until very smooth and fluffy. Let stand a few minutes; check consistency; adjust liquid as needed. Will not be stiff enough to hold a piped or spooned shape

FILLING

Cool doughnuts completely on a cooling rack before filling and/or topping.

For a filled doughnut (jelly, custard, fruit, lemon, chocolate), use the same amount of dough as in the cutout, but make a ball and fry both sides to golden brown. Let cool completely. Use a chopstick to make a hole into the side of the donut. Twist around gently to make space for filling. Using a decorating bag or cone (page 262) and round opening tip, insert into the hole and fill. Place back on cooling rack and top however you like.

GLAZING AND/OR TOPPING

Put parchment/wax paper under cooling rack. Glaze with a variety of choices. For example, try Powdered Sugar Drizzle/Icing—plain or with any added flavor—or Chocolate Pastry Glaze, or honey. Top with sifted powdered sugar, cinnamon-sugar, nutmeg-sugar, sprinkles, bacon, or maple syrup.

MISS CHARLOTTE

PECAN STICKY BUNS & LOAF

Makes 24 muffin-sized buns, 2 loaves, or one Bundt

Make Doughnut dough (recipe on page 186) through the first rise, and the first fold. Do not cut the dough in half; let it rest for 10 minutes, covered with floured plastic.

Make Nut Mix
⅛ c shortening/melted butter
⅓ c brown sugar
⅛ c chopped pecans
1½ t cinnamon
½ c whole pecans

TO MAKE NUT MIX

Blend together melted shortening/butter, brown sugar, pecans, and cinnamon in a medium mixing bowl.

When Doughnut dough has rested 10 minutes, cut in the Nut Mix using a pastry knife, scraper, or a knife until roughly combined in 1–2" chunks. Divide in half.

TO MAKE BUNS

Grease or line a muffin pan. Drop one whole pecan in the bottom of each one.

Drop in enough chunks of the Doughnut dough mixture to fill each cup to ¾ full. Set in proof spot to rise just above the edge of the cup; use the "dimple test" to confirm that the rise is done. (For details on proofing, see Bread Notes, page 269; for Dimple Test, page 271.)

Before the end of the final rise, preheat oven to 350°F.

Note: Make sure you bake these until deep golden brown and hollow-sounding when tapped. They'll be soggy on the bottom if not baked enough!

Bake at 350°F, until a golden brown, about 35–40 minutes.

Cool for about 5 minutes until buns can be gently tilted out of the pan and onto a cooling rack (upside down) without compressing. Cool 10 minutes more on the rack with paper towels underneath. Drizzle generously with the slightly cooled but still very warm Pecan Glaze (page 195).

MISS CHARLOTTE

TO MAKE LOAVES

Grease pan(s). Dot the bottom of the pan with whole pecans. Drop half of the Doughnut dough mixture into each pan. Set in proof spot to rise just above the edge of the pan; use the Dimple Test to confirm that the rise is done. (For details on proofing, see Bread Notes, page 269; for dimple test, page 271.)

Bake at 350°F, until a deep golden brown, about 45–50 minutes. See note about timing.

Cool for about 10 minutes, until loaves can be gently tilted out of the pans and onto a cooling rack (upside down) without compressing. Cool 15 minutes more on the rack with paper towels underneath.

Drizzle generously with the slightly cooled but still very warm Pecan Glaze, below.

1½ c brown sugar
1½ c granulated sugar
1 c salted butter
⅔ c Karo syrup
⅔ c honey
½ c water

WHILE BUNS OR LOAVES ARE BAKING, MAKE PECAN GLAZE

In a medium sauce pan, combine brown sugar, granulated sugar, butter, syrup, honey, and water. Heat until very thick, stirring often.

Drizzle generously over sticky buns and loaves!

MISS CHARLOTTE

BISCUITS

When I think of Charlotte and food, I think of sweets. But she did love a great biscuit. If she needed a morsel of savory food, she often started with one of these pillowy creations, and then she tucked bits of deliciousness inside.

Then she turned her attention to dessert.

Makes about 2 dozen small biscuits
2⅓ c all-purpose flour
3 T granulated sugar
¾ t salt
2½ T baking powder
¼ c milk powder
1 c shortening
¾ c cold water (may use a bit less or more)

Preheat oven to 425°F.

In a medium mixing bowl whisk together all dry ingredients.

Add shortening; mix with two knives or a pastry cutter until crumbly and the shortening is pea-sized pieces.

Make a well in the middle of this mixture, and add ½ c water all at once; mix. Add another ¼ c water—until dough is moist and sticky and just able to form a ball.

Turn dough onto a heavily floured surface or board, and roll to ¾" or desired thickness.

Using a floured cutter or a glass, cut out biscuits and place on a parchment-lined or ungreased baking sheet, 1" apart. You can place them upside down if you want a smooth top. Bake until lightly brown, about 15–20 minutes.

EYDES
WITNESS

CHAPTER 6
SISTERS

Here are my sisters doing what they always did. It kills me how Judi is blocking the sun from my baby face, while Linda holds me up.

Dad always said I was a lucky charm. He's referring to the fact that I was born the year he started over again—with the Alexandria bakery, the one he would eventually buy from his father and his brother. The one that became the centerpiece of our family's life.

It's the spring of 1964 and my two sisters and I are in the back of the light brown station wagon. We're at the drive-in movie, and our parents are in the front seat, sitting close. The bright light flickers through the windshield and flutters around in the car. My sisters and I are cozy in our pajamas, in the way-back with the seat down so we can all three can lie down, filling

A BAKER'S DAUGHTER

the humid space with sweet, clean bathtub smells. I remember it like it was yesterday. Linda and Judi are jumping around the car playing, and I'm lying on my back. I can't yet walk or talk, but I can wiggle. The wheel well is bigger than me and looms in a half circle of plastic alongside me. A greasy smell sneaks out of the seam where the silver lever closure snaps it shut. The light from the movie screen flashes and swirls with the scenes, filtering through our handprints on the foggy glass. The sisters make drippy shapes with their fingers on the dewy surface. I hear voices crackling from the fat, square speaker, hooked on the driver's-side window next to my dad's head.

My sisters aren't watching the movie; instead, I'm the star of their movie. They're laughing, playing with me, kissing me, making baby noises, touching me, holding me up. Our parents are watching the screen, lost together in their grown-up world, knowing that we're fine. Letting us just be fine without them. The backs of their heads are a silhouette, my mom's curl-flip on one side of her hair, happiness in her buck-toothed profile when she smiles at our dad.

This is my first memory, and the memory that defines our family. It's the memory that defines my life.

My sisters are eight and twelve years older than I. There's a photo of them holding me when I was just days old. It's black and white with the border stamped with the date, August 1963. Judi is shielding my head from the sun, which is streaming in through

Linda and Judi in 1958. I don't know if Linda's hair is short here because Judi had already cut off her ponytail, or if that happened sometime later.

the bedroom window through a white sheer curtain. Linda is proudly smiling down on me. This would define how they held me my whole life, long after I outgrew their preteen arms. With tenderness and loving kindness. My protectors. They doted on me and loved me without end; they still do. I was their baby.

I would also become the peacemaker of the family. We needed one at the time, because just around the time I came into the world, Judi cut Linda's pony tail off in her sleep. I think it changed their relationship forever, and they needed something else to focus on. I was that thing, and I felt my destiny. I did my damnedest to be perky and fun, and to encourage everyone to be understanding and loving to one another. It was a tough gig, and certainly, as it turned out, a misguided attempt. It turned out that my peacekeeping was really just a way to create order in my own life. As it turns out, I am Charlotte's daughter after all.

My sisters were my first friends, caregivers; my friendly witnesses. I received an unconditional love from them that has sustained me all my life. Their love remains a hum in my ear that's constant, a sound I'd miss it if it were to stop, like evening insect songs I still feel them holding me, taking me with them wherever they went. I don't remember ever crying, because they were always there to take care of me, pick me up and distract my tears, change my diapers. My baby feet never touched the ground.

In the kitchen at our dining table, I remember sitting in my high chair, watching the interaction of my family. One night, my sisters fed me bourbon, and I started laughing. I didn't stop. I couldn't stop. My sisters giggled uncontrollably when mom asked, "What did you do to that child?" And that made them laugh even more. Later, they didn't think it's so funny when I finger-painted my room with the contents of my diaper. Mom had a quick gag reflex, so they were left to clean it up. I will never live that down.

By the time I came along, Mom obviously knew what she was going to know about raising kids—but so much time had passed, she picked up Dr. Spock, just to refresh her memory. I remember her Southern voice as she read story books to me. She and Dad took me along to watch from the chilly bleachers when Linda twirled fire batons to the soundtrack from "Shaft," for the half-time program during the local high school football game. Linda's majorette team would let me attend their practices and step along.

When her boyfriend—and future husband, Harry Sherman—would visit the house, I would sit right between them. They were kind to me, but if I wouldn't leave them alone, eventually she would pretend to call our family doctor and ask him to come give me a shot. My first plane trip was to Cookville, Tennessee, to visit Linda and Harry after they married.

In those days people "dressed" to fly in an airplane. Mom sewed me a two-piece "travel outfit" made out of burnt red 100-percent wool. The tunic had long sleeves and was embellished with gold tassels around the neck. The pants, also wool, were bell-bottomed and fringed with gold at the bottom.

It was mod and fantastic. It was also hot and scratchy and 100-percent agonizing.

But it was worth it, because in the Nashville airport, I met Johnny Cash. He must have been seven feet tall that day, a dark, larger-than-life tree of a man dressed in black, with dirt in the creases of his forehead. I saw those creases when he bent way down to hand me back the only piece of paper I had for the autograph—a picture of me with Santa Claus.

Next, I became a drill team mascot for Judi, complete with the uniform and school "E" letter on my sweater, red pom-poms on my saddle oxfords. When Mom read a sex education book to me, I was left with questions I could ask only Judi. Thankfully, she explained how things really worked. She told me about menstruation. Boys. When my new puppy died, it was Judi waiting for me to return home from school, wanting to be sure she was the one to tell me. She was my interpreter of real life, a buffer between me and bona fide pain.

She also showed me what real life looked like—driving around in her 1967 Ford Mustang, yellow with a black cloth hard top. I'd sit in the back seat, often with one of my little friends. She and whoever was riding shotgun would cruise around our town, smoking cigarettes, burning incense, talking their teenage talk about boys and school. She even took me to parties. I made extra money extorting Judi so I wouldn't tell our parents—but really, I never would have. I was safe with Judi and I knew it.

Then they were gone.

I became an only child of an "older couple" who had reached financial stability, if not upper-middle-class affluence. By the time I was this child, my parents were touching their dreams. I was still toted along for the ride, but now to restaurants and parties where I'd fall asleep in a booth under a linen napkin. I hung out with adults and their friends. I found out that older people were fun and knew stuff my peers didn't. I found out that farts are funny at every age. I heard dirty jokes and double entendres, and read all the books on the shelf—including several I had no business reading. I eavesdropped on the adult conversations going on around me.

All of that kid-sized solitude, without siblings, gifted me with a love of aloneness, inner self-awareness, imagination, and independence. All of that quiet allowed me to reach inside in a way that would never have happened without extended alone-time. It fueled my love of words and music.

And without my sisters, I eventually became that teenager with the pool. She lived by the river and water skied and drank whiskey. She did gymnastics and straightened her hair and had tall boyfriends.

NEW BEGINNINGS

My family knows a lot about starting over. My grandparents took the leap across the ocean to escape certain misery, to escape the

death that surrounded them. Once people got settled, the various Brenners went off on their own, starting their own bakeries. My dad, younger than most of them, finally broke away from his father and brothers to start the doughnut shop. After he hit bottom there, he rejoined the family, gathered himself, and launched again. When he took over "our" bakery, he turned it into something that could sustain us.

My sisters and I learned that starting over is a way of life.

When Dad and I are talking about this, he reflects for a moment, and counts off the husbands. "Of the eight weddings for three daughters, I've made six wedding cakes!" he laughs, subtracting the elopement and the wedding that was too far away for him to bake. His laugh holds reflection, disappointment, hope, humanity, and unadulterated humor. It holds the circle of life. This one statement tells so much about the rocky roads of my sisters and me, our belief in love, our transparency, our willingness to be vulnerable, and our stubbornness. We never doubted that Dad would make as many wedding cakes as it would take for us to be happy. We never doubted that we could be happy. We never doubted that we would.

Mom was only twenty when she had Linda, after having been told she wouldn't have any children. Dad recalled that "Linda had colic and cried all night long for what seemed like months." He said she was beautiful and cocky, even in her infancy. The day Judi was born, Linda inadvertently took center stage. She had something lodged in her ear, so Dad was with her at a doctor's office while Mom was giving birth at the hospital. Judi was "an easy baby," night to Linda's day. They were opposites. Linda was the strong side of mom and Judi was the soft, conciliatory side. Mom had a knack for driving them both crazy. By the time I arrived, so many years later, they had broken her in for me.

When Linda got married for the first time, I was her six-year-old flower girl; when Judi left home for college, I was ten. After that, I was raised mostly on my own. I learned to negotiate. I learned to manage. I made my own way. When Judi first got married, I was fourteen. I waved goodbye to her as she drove off with her husband. I was holding their cake top and first layer, along with a bottle of champagne and her engagement ring. My job was to save these precious items for when she returned from her honeymoon. "Hey Jude" was playing on the radio.

Eventually, my sisters gave me a niece and two nephews, my live baby dolls. Linda was first. Her Christine—who is only eight years younger than I—reminds me most of my sweet Aunt Florence; her brother, Jason, would eventually help me solve the mysteries of many of the bakery's recipes. I still remember helping Linda to get their nursery ready. I was there when they came home from the hospital. I was their babysitter. I'd ride my bike over to help feed them, and push them in the swings. Their father, Harry, took over the bakery from my dad, and both kids worked there—but Jason worked in the back. Jason measured and

My little mascots, nephew Jason and niece Christine, in my beanbag chair, 1975.

mixed and baked. Christine helped me reconstruct flavors and textures, and she practiced the recipes with me.

Their presence in that building carried on my father's family tradition. They simply didn't walk through that life alone. Neither did my dad.

"My life has always been filled with family involvement," Dad wrote to me. "All endeavors—whether help or catching hell—eventually included someone in the family. Through it all emerged an endearing respect for the family as a unit of survival."

I watched that family unit grow, the way most families do. My youngest nephew, Jonathan, came along later and lived in Maryland with Judi. In his younger years, we spent many a winter week traveling out to Utah to share our mutual love of skiing. Now these "babies" are giving me great-nieces and -nephews to cherish. The beat goes on. It always does.

"BRENNER GIRLS HAVE NICE BUNS"

This was but one common pun repeated by our friends about us baker's daughters. We took it in stride for a couple of reasons. The first was that it was a time before the #MeToo movement, and we wanted nice buns. The second was that we were the kids with the bakery. Say what you will; we were the lucky ones.

Frankly, we might have been lucky, but we were imperfect employees. Linda and Judi shared Mom's difficulties in counting back change and I ate more than I sold. My friends thought I had

Judi, Dad, and me, in the kitchen, 1966.

a hollow leg, but I frequently made myself sick by eating only bakery goodies during my after-school shift, from three until close, at nine. I was responsible for my dinner, and rarely would I eat a real dinner. There was a grocery store, as well as a steak house in the shopping center, but…I was a teenager.

Each of us three sisters has a different experience of the bakery. Our own version of the same bones of a story. If we each were to fill a white box with our absolute favorites, they'd be different—but together, they created a particular set of recipes that we favored. This chapter celebrates us girls, and what we craved for our most special occasions.

There were a few things we all loved. The first was birthday cake. Of course, one perk of being a "Brenner Girl" was to be able to pick whatever kind of cake we wanted. Dad custom-decorated, and we chose toppers from the cake case. Linda's favorite was one made like a giant Petit Four. Judi always wanted the ballerina that moved on a base. I loved the ballerinas that held candles, and the sugar blue birds. Those looked best on a yellow cake with white icing. When I was older, it was Boston cream pie, and Dad would write "happy birthday" on it.

I've considered the truth that every family has its stories, along with some kind of glue that holds it together. Sometimes people fade away, or break off all together—but usually, there's something familiar that makes a family into a recognizable, chaotic, unruly, unpredictable unit. I see us Brenner Girls as ingredients. Maybe

the sugar and spices in a pumpkin pie; maybe the sticky buns or fruit pies themselves, or the savory breads. I see our family as being held together with egg wash or icing or—on a fancy day, a wedding day—rosettes. Maybe we're blended together and maybe we're stacked on a plastic tray, peering out from a glass case. Whatever we are, we were put together with the tears and laughter of generations of our ancestors, of the boat ride from Europe, the broken wagon, the whispered Yiddish, the games of cards and the horse races and hay ride and buck teeth. We were made from skinny-dipping in the pool.

And just as the Brenner Girls had nice buns, and were imperfect employees, we were also only human. We were made from bodies that carried mutations to both BRCA1 and BRCA2, the breast cancer genes that can make your whole body want to die. When our mother was dying, her cancer focused on her ovaries. We daughters cared for her together, as much as we each could. We were forever-sisters in those months. It was Linda—our elder leader—who paged me at the airport, so I could get right back on the plane when Charlotte died. It was Judi—my fiercest protector—who stayed with me only three years later, during my twelve-week bone-marrow transplant.

It seemed like only an instant after my mother died when I was faced with my first diagnosis of advanced breast cancer. I was thirty-four. Dad, my Max, my best friend—after just losing his beloved wife of fifty years—came over every morning to do my dishes, make food for me, and take me to doctor's appointments. And yes, both sisters came to help. Again, my feet never touched the ground. The only time I ever cried was when I feared that the damn disease might strike them, too. I held on to the notion that if I could survive this, perhaps I could gain knowledge that would save them from ever having to go through it. They helped me to save my life. Without them, I wouldn't be me. I wouldn't be here.

"THE REST OF THE STORY"

As I reflect on how our family's story is told through breaking bread and our collective history, I also realize that each of us has his or her own life. We have had our singular experiences, ones that contribute to our individuality. Many of my first independent recollections—moments without my sisters—usually revolved around music.

Maybe it's because music is my native tongue, but being around Max was like being around a whistling juke box. To me, music was part of my bones; it was part of each day; it was embedded in certain environments. On early-morning drives, when I sometimes went along with him to the bakery, the only time he stopped whistling was when he listened to talk radio. He was hooked on the news and stories, and he especially loved Paul Harvey. I quickly learned the Souza marches that opened his radio show. "That wakes me up!" Dad would say. To this day, a Souza march still wakes me up.

I also can recall the short theme music that opened the news—no matter where I am, any vintage jingle recalls it: "Bah bah bah, bah-dah…" This music punctuated my day—because Mrs. Van Scoyoc also listened to talk radio when we went to pick up her eldest son from school. Mrs. Van Scoyoc (I'm supposed to call her Nancy now) was our across-the-street neighbor before I was school-age. When Charlotte was at work, I spent days with her—and her youngest son, David, who would become my first non-family, truly close person.

These two people are the architects of some of my most precious memories. David and I were just three when we met, and Nancy would toss us both into the blue station wagon. We'd be eating peanut butter and jelly in the back seat—and she'd cut the radio on. Again, I'd hear the pre-news music bit there every day. "Bah bah bah, bah-dah…" Even today, when I hear that music, I taste peanut butter. I am right back there, sitting next to David, with the breeze coming in the open window, smelling the smell of the old station wagon, all oil and gas and upholstery.

Nancy was also a role model for me. She was the first instrument-playing musician I ever met. She played the piano and the flute, and I remember becoming mesmerized with her in action. I could not get enough of her fingers on the keys, or the way her breath was so light and variable on the flute. She transformed physical objects so that they *became* the music. She ignited my lifelong passion.

Top: This photo of Max's "apprentice," my brother-in-law Harry, reminds me of a similar shot of Big Bubbe (page 18). Although Harry wasn't born a Brenner, he sure acted like one! Bottom: With Rose, who also worked for years with Max at the same location.

I still listen to talk radio, a habit from Nancy and Dad, but there are no more marches and no more Paul Harvey. Still, the essence of those shows makes me listen for my dad's whistle.

And without my dad—and his whistle, for that matter—Brenner's Bakery discovered its own future. It remained in Alexandria—in the same spot—from 1953 until 2004. However, by the fast-paced 1980s, things started changing in specialty shops; the writing was on the wall. When folks began to make only one stop for their groceries, a real bakery couldn't compete with the low prices of the high-volume-production baked goods at supermarkets. Harry did a great job of running things after Dad retired. He also worked with Five Guys to help develop their pizza and roll dough, and remains a bakery consultant for them. But Brenner's lost the foot race. The bakery was finally sold out of the family, passed through several hands, and then faded away.

Since then, the world has changed again. People are rediscovering specialty shops, sitting in coffee shops to work and visit, and spending time with baked goods. At the time of this writing, Markos Panas is operating a beautiful bakery/restaurant in the old Belle View, Alexandria, location—called Bread & Water Company. And in further synchronicity, he has recently opened at least one location in Arlington, Virginia.

The new bakery's name startled me when I first heard it. I had written the Bread and Water chapter about my grandfather many years ago, long before I met Markos Panas. It appears that

our families are connected by that sweet, historied space. I've truly appreciated getting to know the Panas family, and I rejoice in their successes.

After his retirement, and my mother's death, my dad also had some personal experiences—experiences that served him as a person, and yet did not take him away from his connection to his daughters. As it turned out, Max's ability to love didn't end with us—or with Charlotte. For some eighteen years, he and a gentle, smart, and organized woman named Barbara had a beautiful life together, until Dad died on February 21, 2017. They were a living example of the endless energy and power of hope, and the capacity to connect. Max was always a living demonstration of the possibility of intimacy. Love always answered him. It talked to him. It held him. It nurtured him. Today, Barbara, along with Charlotte's brother Alan, are our family's only living representatives of that generation. This book is also their legacy.

I grew up to be a business person, musician, public speaker, and writer. As a performing songwriter, my work starts when a baker would be heading for bed. There is not a single late night when I don't think of my dad. This is because of another experience I got to have—one that no one else on earth ever even knew about. Except Max.

As the only sister to have her own car at sixteen, I tended to partake in surreptitious teenaged outings. As the "evenings" wound down, I staged my approach the big house by the river—in my metallic green Oldsmobile Starfire. I would drive back with the windows open, to blow the smoke smell out of my clothes. I would pop a fresh piece of gum in my mouth, after racing the Fort Belvoir boys at stop lights in my beast of a car. I would park, quietly shut my car door, and carefully open the house door, working hard to avoid making a sound. Working hard to avoid waking Mom.

On most of those early mornings, I would meet Dad on the gold-carpeted stairs. It would be 3 a.m. I'd be on my way up—sneaking in past my curfew—and he'd be on his way down, on his way to work. We both would pause.

"Morning, Daddy," I'd whisper to him in the dark.

He would kiss me with his firm whistler lips, all toothpaste and shaving-cream clean. I could see his wide smile in the dark, feel his eyes sparkle.

"Good night, Baby."

Above: Our family portrait, circa 1966. Sister Linda stands in the back; seated from left, Charlotte, Dad; Judi and I are in front. Dig the hairdos.
Opposite page: The family after Charlotte left us, with Linda on the left and Judi on the right, 2011.

A BAKER'S DAUGHTER

SISTERS

BROWNIES

At the bakery, these brownies were always displayed and boxed with wax paper underneath, and now I know why.

Makes about 16–24 squares
1¼ c all-purpose flour
pinch of salt
1 c shortening
2⅛ c brown sugar
1 c chocolate fudge base (or more, if icing; see page 258 for fudge base)
½ c corn syrup (Karo)
4 eggs
1½ t vanilla extract
1 c chopped walnuts (chop then measure)

PREPARATION

Lightly oil or line with parchment the baking pan of your choice (see note). Preheat oven to 350°F.

In a mixing bowl, combine flour and salt; set aside. In another bowl—either standing mixer or by hand—cream butter. Scrape sides of bowl and beater.

To butter, add brown sugar, fudge base, corn syrup, and vanilla, mixing until smooth. Scrape sides of bowl and beater.

Add eggs one at a time. With each addition, cream together until combined and smooth, for a minute or less, scraping sides of bowl and beater.

Add the dry ingredient mixture, ⅓ at a time, until combined and smooth. Scrape sides of the bowl and the beater.

Add walnuts; mix briefly until combined.

Scrape batter into your prepared pan, leveling it out.

Note on pan sizes:
To achieve a thinner brownie like the bakery's, use a half sheet (12" x 18") baking pan. For a thicker, more traditional brownie, use a 9" x 13" baking pan. If you don't have a half-sheet pan, you can divide the batter between two 9" x 13" pans to achieve the thinner brownie result.

BAKING & TOPPING

Bake at 350 for about 28–30 minutes if half-sheet; 40 minutes for thicker. A toothpick test in the middle helps you gauge, but be careful not to over bake. Brownies should be just set and not "jiggly" in the center. Edges and corners should be firm.

Place on a cooling rack until completely cool.

Place a baking sheet or cutting board over the brownie pan. Flip the whole pan over, popping the brownie onto the sheet/board.

Sprinkle enough granulated sugar into the original baking pan to completely coat the bottom. Then, using your hand and arm, carefully flip the brownie back into the sugar-lined pan. Lightly press it down into the pan to coat the bottom with the sugar.

SISTERS

SERVING VARIATIONS:

NAKED:
Using a warm knife/scraper, slice into bars of desired size and place onto a wax paper-lined serving plate or into a storage container.

FULL-OCTANE FUDGE:
At the bakery, we used the fudge base straight up. Warm it gradually in the microwave, a few seconds at a time, or place in a bowl of warm water, until easily spreadable. Go for it: spread to a ¼" layer on top of the brownie.

CHOCOLATE FUDGE ICING:
This variation of Chocolate Fudge Icing uses the balance of a 12-oz. tub of fudge base (after the brownie recipe's 1c has been removed). Simply blend ingredients and spread.

Mix all ingredients with a standing mixer or by hand until very smooth and it turns fluffy and spreadable. Let stand a few minutes, and then give it a quick mix to check consistency. Add more milk or water to adjust, a little at a time.

This recipe is the way I remember it, on the bittersweet side, but you can adjust the amount of sugar to desired sweetness. If you shift sugar quantities, you might have to add a bit more liquid, too. Note: sugar also shifts the color a bit.

The icing should be moist and soft enough to pipe, but still be very fudgy and firm enough to hold the drop shape on top of the Butter Cookie. The icing will set on the outside when dry, but stay moist inside, just like Brenner's.

Chocolate Fudge Icing
⅓ c fudge base (see page 258)
2 c powdered sugar
⅛ t vanilla extract
⅛ t water

APPLE CINNAMON NUT LOAF

Makes two loaves
Make Doughnut dough (recipe on page 186) through the first rise, and the first fold. Cut the dough in half; let it rest for 10 minutes, covered with floured plastic.

2 T cinnamon
½ c brown sugar
⅛ t ground nutmeg
1 c chopped walnuts
2½ c fresh apples (about 4 small apples, diced small)

In a mixing bowl, combine cinnamon, brown sugar, nutmeg, walnuts, and apples. Set aside.

Grease pan(s).

Press or roll out one half the dough to about 2" thick. Layer half of the cinnamon/apple mixture on top of the dough, then roll up and chop into 1–2" pieces. I know it sounds weird, but just kind of mix the pieces around as you chop—don't "blend" or work the dough. This is very messy! Put the mixture into a greased loaf pan. Do the same with the other half.

Set in a warm place, covered with plastic, to rise to puffy and "one thumb knuckle" above the rim of the loaf pan. Use the Dimple Test to confirm that the rise is done. (For details on proofing, see Bread Notes, page 169; for Dimple Test, page 171.)

Before the end of the final rise, preheat the oven to 350°F.

Bake at 350°F for about 30–40 minutes until deep golden brown. See note on timing.

Timing note:
Bake until deep golden brown and hollow-sounding when tapped. Otherwise, sides and bottom will be undercooked.

Powdered Sugar Drizzle/Icing
6+ c powdered sugar (measure then sift)
⅓+ c milk or water (a little at a time)
⅛ c (2 T) vanilla extract

Mix ingredients. To achieve a pourable consistency, you might need a bit more liquid.

Let cool in the pan before gently tilting out, upside down, onto a cooling rack. When completely cool, flip loaves right-side-up, and place parchment or wax paper underneath the drying rack. Although it's optional, "everyone" drizzles icing on top, letting it run down the sides and into the pockets on top.

If you attempt to slice before loaves are cool, they might compress and be difficult to cut. Be patient!

CHOCOLATE ÉCLAIRS

Makes about 2 dozen
1 c shortening
2 c water
2¼ c bread flour
1 T baking powder
2 t salt
8 eggs
Vanilla Custard (page 168)

STEP 1 PREPARATION
Spray a baking sheet with oil and then line with parchment. This keeps the parchment from slipping while you pipe out your Éclairs.

In a medium mixing bowl, combine flour, salt, and baking powder; set aside.

In a large saucepan, combine water and shortening. Heat at medium until butter melts and water reaches a boil. Remove pan from heat.

Preheat oven to 425°F.

Add dry mixture all at once to the heated mixture and stir vigorously with a wooden spoon until well blended.

Return to low heat and cook, stirring constantly with a smearing motion, until mixture is 170–175°F, follows the spoon around the pan and looks like shiny mashed potatoes (about a minute or less).

Emergency Éclair notes:
Éclair/puff shells—
You can make these ahead. Just store at room temperature—either covered or in a paper bag—with plenty of space between them. Definitely do not stack them tightly, as they get soggy. If your stored puffs do get soggy, then re-crisp in the oven at 375°F for 10 minutes or so. Cool completely before filling.

Vanilla Custard filling—
Also can be stored in the fridge until using.

STEP 2 PREPARATION
Immediately transfer mixture into the standing mixer bowl. Using a whisk attachment, or food processor with feed tube open, or by hand, mix for 10–15 seconds to start the mixture cooling. Allow it to rest and cool to 125°F. It will be hot but you can hold a finger in it for a few seconds.

With the mixer (level 2) running, add eggs in a steady stream, all at one time. Scrape the bowl and whisk when all in, then beat for another 2 minutes.

SISTERS

Chocolate Pastry Glaze
Makes about a quart
(32 oz., 2#)
1⅓ c chocolate fudge base (one 12-oz. container, see page 258)
¾ t vanilla extract
6+ c powdered sugar (measure then sift)
1 c milk or water (don't use all at once)

Mix ingredients until very smooth and fluffy. Let stand a few minutes; check consistency; adjust liquid as needed. Will not be stiff enough to hold a piped or spooned shape.

Note: Chocolate Pastry Glaze can be stored in the fridge; just let it reach room temperature or warm it a few seconds in the microwave before use.

FINISHING & BAKING
To form an Éclair, pipe batter out into a log approximately 5" long and ½–1" thick. Or, use a scoop or big spoon to drop the batter in a 3–4T mound to create a round, cream puff shape. Use the back of a spoon to smooth the top. (For details on how to make a piping bag, see Cookie Techniques on page 262.)

Bake for 15 minutes at 425°F, then reduce the heat to 375°F until golden brown and fairly firm, about 25 minutes if Éclairs are on the large side like the bakery's. DO NOT OPEN THE OVEN DURING BAKING!

Turn off oven.

FILLING & ICING
Quickly take Éclairs/puffs out of oven, and close oven door immediately. With a sharp knife, make a small slit on top of each Éclair/puff and return to oven. Let them stay in the cooling oven for at least 10–15 minutes to let the steam escape, and then place them on a rack to cool.

Assemble the Éclairs when they're close to being served so they don't get soggy.

Use a chop stick to make a hole on each end (Éclairs), or in the side (puffs), gently rolling the stick around on the interior to make space for the filling. Then pipe Vanilla Custard into the Éclair using a decorator bag and a small round tip.

Ice tops with Chocolate Pastry Glaze. *Et voilà!.*

SISTERS

BOSTON CREAM PIE

It's not really a pie. But it's not a cake either. It's Yellow Layer Cake with Vanilla Custard Filling topped with Chocolate Fudge Icing—all the best things wrapped into one. Boston Cream Pies were in the refrigerated case along with Chocolate Éclairs.

This was my favorite birthday cake. The waxy candles would push through the chilled chocolate into the yellow layer cake. The blended taste of yellow cake, vanilla custard, and chocolate is the flavor of my childhood itself, and always tied to celebrations. A Boston Cream Pie is an occasion for something special. It probably deserves its own holiday.

Makes one pie/cake
Yellow Layer Cake, chilled (page 138)
Vanilla Custard, preferably made the night before use (page 168)

PREPARATION

Spread Custard about ½" thick on top of one cake layer.

Spread Chocolate Fudge Icing about ¼" thick on top of the other cake layer.

Refrigerate the layers for 30 minutes.

Once chilled, place the chocolate layer on top of the custard layer, "gooey sides up." Refrigerate until serving. Use a warmed knife to slice through the cold layers.

Chocolate Fudge Icing
Makes about a quart
(32 oz., 2#)
1⅓ c chocolate fudge base (one 12-oz. container, see page 258)
¾ t vanilla extract
6+ c powdered sugar (measure then sift)
¾+ c milk or water (don't use all at once)

CHOCOLATE FUDGE ICING

Mix all ingredients with a standing mixer or by hand until very smooth and just turns fluffy and spreadable. Let it stand a few minutes, give it a quick mix and then check again, as it may need a bit more liquid. Add more milk or water to adjust, a little at a time.

This recipe is the way I remember it, on the bittersweet side—but you can adjust the amount of sugar to desired sweetness. If you shift sugar quantities, you might have to add a bit more liquid, too. Note: sugar also shifts the color a bit.

PETIT FOURS

This is the cake that my sister Linda would ask for on *her* birthday. (And who could blame her?) It's a variation on the Yellow Pound Cake recipe.

Makes about 72 small cakes (one bite each for some, two bites for me)
Yellow Pound Cake, 9" x 13" half-sheet, cool (page 132)
jelly or preserves

PREPARATION

Cut the Pound Cake in half. One half at a time, place on a surface and cut horizontally into two layers. For tools and tips on how to do this more easily, see Cake Techniques, page 264.

Spread a thin layer (maybe ¼") of jelly or preserves on top of one layer, and place the other layer on top of the filling. Chill for at least an hour before the next step.

Cut into 1½" squares of layer cake and place on a cooling rack with wax paper underneath.

Powdered Sugar Drizzle/Icing
6+ c powdered sugar (measure then sift)
⅓+ c milk or water (a little at a time)
⅛ c (2 T) vanilla extract

To create a pourable consistency, you might need a bit more liquid.

Buttercream Icing
1⅓ c shortening
12+ c powdered sugar (measure then sift)
4 t vanilla extract
⅔ c water or milk (room temperature)

ICING & DECORATING

Generously cover each square with thick drizzle icing, so the entire exposed cake is coated. Allow to set, about 30 minutes.

Decorate with buttercream icing, edible decorations, fruit, or anything you can imagine.

BUTTERCREAM ICING PREPARATION

Beat half the shortening until fluffy. Add half the powdered sugar and blend. Add vanilla and half the water and beat until combined. Continue adding sugar and water, alternating until incorporated. Beat until light and fluffy.

The frosting should be easily spreadable. If it's too "loose" for decorating, then make it stiffer by adding a bit more sugar.

GINGERBREAD CAKE

One 9" x 13" cake or about 24 cupcakes
1½ c shortening
2⅛ c brown sugar
1 egg
¾ c molasses
5½ c cake flour
(sifted then measured)
1½ T baking soda
1 T salt
2⅛ t ground ginger
¾ t allspice
¾ c cold water

PREPARATION

Bring all ingredients to room temperature, except water. Grease and flour pan(s). Preheat oven to 325°F.

In a medium mixing bowl, stir together flour, baking soda, salt, ginger, and allspice; set aside. In another bowl—either standing mixer or by hand—beat shortening so it's light and fluffy, about 30 seconds.

Add sugar, beat another 30 seconds to cream, scrape sides of bowl and beater. Add eggs one at a time, beating only enough to incorporate. After each one, scrape sides and beater.

Add dry mixture and water alternately, about ⅓ of each at a time. After each addition, beat only until combined, and s crape down sides. Batter will be silky. Do not over beat!

Blend in molasses and then vanilla. After each, scrape sides.

No matter what pan you're using, pour batter to fill to ⅔.

Bake 60–65 minutes for cake, less for cupcakes. Bake until toothpick or knife comes out clean from the center. Cake will bounce back from a gentle touch.

Cool cake or cupcakes in pan on a rack until cool enough to tilt out; finish cooling on rack.

When completely cool, ice with Chocolate Fudge Icing. If icing gets firm in the fridge, then use a warmed knife to cut the cake.

Chocolate Fudge Icing
Makes about a quart (32 oz., 2#)
1⅓ c fudge base (one 12-oz. container; see page 158)
¾ t vanilla extract
6+ c powdered sugar (measure then sift)
¾+ c milk or water (don't use all at once)

CHOCOLATE FUDGE ICING PREPARATION

Mix all ingredients with a standing mixer or by hand until very smooth and just turns fluffy and spreadable. Let it stand a few minutes, give it a quick mix and then check again, as it may need a bit more liquid. Add more milk or water to adjust, a little at a time.

This recipe is the way I remember it, on the bittersweet side—but you can adjust the amount of sugar to desired sweetness. If you shift sugar quantities, you might have to add a bit more liquid, too. Note: sugar also shifts the color a bit.

RADIO BARS

All three of us sisters craved Radio Bars. After Chocolate Top Cookies, these were our favorite—these irresistible fingers of devil's food cake with white icing spiraling over the top, all covered in chocolate. A Radio Bar was the first thing to put me over the edge of eating more than I sold. It was during a night shift, and I chose a third one over a steak dinner. I recommend including protein in a meal of Radio Bars, as too many of them can produce a stomach ache in a teenager. All three of us girls both loved and hated them.

There is no ingredient card for Radio Bars, but you can still make them

Devil's Food / chocolate layer cake, square chocolate syrup (see note)

PREPARATION

Buy or bake a chocolate ("devil's food") layer cake of your choice, preferably in a square cake pan.

When completely cooled, cut the cake into rectangles, about 5" x 1½". Place them on a cookie cooling rack.

Pipe or spoon Vanilla Buttercream Icing in a fat swirl along the top of the rectangle of chocolate cake.

Make or buy a rich chocolate syrup (see note), and pour it over the confection of cake and icing to completely cover it.

It may not be exactly the same as Brenner's, but it'll be good!

Buttercream Icing
1 ⅓ c shortening
12+ c powdered sugar
(measure then sift)
4 t vanilla extract
⅔ c water or milk
(room temp)

Chocolate syrup methods:
You can simply buy a premade, thick syrup, or make one yourself. To easily make, add water or milk to Chocolate Pastry Glaze to syrup consistency.

Chocolate Pastry Glaze (syrup base)
Makes about a quart
(32 oz., 2#)
1 ⅓ c chocolate fudge base (one 12-oz. container, see page 258)
¾ t vanilla extract
6+ c powdered sugar
(measure then sift)
1+ c milk or water
(don't use all at once)

BUTTERCREAM ICING PREPARATION
Beat half the shortening until fluffy. Add half the powdered sugar and blend. Add vanilla and half the water and beat until combined. Continue adding sugar and water, alternating until incorporated. Beat until light and fluffy.

The frosting should be easily spreadable. If it's too "loose" for decorating, then make it stiffer by adding a bit more sugar.

MAKING CHOCOLATE SYRUP WITH CHOCOLATE PASTRY GLAZE
Mix ingredients at left until very smooth and fluffy. Let stand a few minutes. Check consistency, and add additional liquid until glaze becomes a thick syrup.

SISTERS

EPILOGUE
MARCY, FROM THE OUTSIDE IN

By Kristin Donnan

Our twentieth high school reunion was held the same year Marcy underwent stem-cell replacement, after her second breast cancer diagnosis. Even though we were a year apart, we'd been friends with all the same kids, so "my" crowd was her crowd. We went together. She brought her fatigue, bald head, and a wig made from her own luscious hair. Sometimes she wore the wig, and sometimes she didn't. I brought answers, so that people didn't ask her so many questions.

Before the stem-cell procedure, I loved Marcy's approach to dealing with the possibility of death as an outcome. She flipped over her artwork and wrote the names of people who "co-owned" the pieces—so as to make it easy for her sisters to manage how to distribute them, if necessary. She used her business-administration brain, and had every document in order; every eventuality laid out. She wasn't thrilled with her situation—especially after nursing her mother through cancer—but she wasn't going to fall for its morose line of doom, either.

Above: A portrait soon after the first mastectomy, February 1998.
Opposite page:
Top: Her husband, Louis ("pronounced the French way"), doing what he does.
Bottom: Their precious daughter, Charlotte, named after Marcy's mother.

A few years before, I'd been to a Relay for Life with Max and Marcy, after her mom and my dad had both died of cancer. I'd talked through the end of her second marriage—when her husband left while she was in treatment the first time. I'd seen her manage. She always manages.

And then she got sick. Again. Marcy got sick because she has mutations to both breast cancer genes. All women have these genes, which, when functioning well, repair cell damage and keep breast, ovarian, and other cells growing normally. Shortly after she survived stem-cell replacement—a thirty- to fifty-percent chance—Marcy wanted to have all her "female-related" cells removed, to minimize the possibility of more cancer. It's the same surgery Angelina Jolie would have. I remember when Marcy explained what her surgeon had said. She relayed it with the Charlotte's hand-me-down chuckle: "He said if I don't die of brain cancer in two years, then he'll do it, but he doesn't want me to have a bunch of surgery if I won't be here very long."

A year later, she removed everything that hadn't already been removed. Her final surgery was in 2001. As of this writing, she is alive nearly 20 years later—and speaks to cancer groups, often sharing songs and videos she's published about her experience. She didn't get breast reconstructions, and engages in interesting conversations with lawyers—you know, in coffee shops or at the beach—about whether they think that a female person without breasts is obligated to wear a bathing-suit top in public.

So what does a person like that do, after assuming she will die a few times—and then she doesn't? She builds a new life, falls in love again, writes and performs songs, builds a music venue with her husband, continues to laugh the signature laugh—and considers writing about her dad.

And then Charlotte came along. Not her mother Charlotte, but a little girl born to a young woman who could not keep her. Marcy had long ago reconciled with the fact that she would never have natural children—but wondered if she should ever take on the responsibility of parenthood. It's a fair question, for people who have written other people's names on the backs of the art hanging on their walls. When little Charlotte appeared, it was as if all of Marcy's ancestors—on both sides—clicked onto a paranormal conference call. Generations of gamblers—generations of people who risked life and limb, or at least their fortunes and happiness—whispered in her ear. And Marcy did what Marcy does. She said yes.

Turns out that little Charlotte was born with a mutation, too. She had Phelan McDermid Syndrome, an illness that can manifest with delayed development and an array of other symptoms, including seizures. It's different in every child, and so prognoses differ significantly—but children with this chromosomal malformation can have shortened life spans. The new mama loved Charlotte exactly as much as if they would both live forever. It was beautiful to see Marcy naturally adapt

EPILOGUE

to motherhood. It was as if she simply stepped into a new life and never looked back. As usual, Marcy was all-in. So was her husband Lou; they had a daughter. It was a miracle.

Until the day when it wasn't. One morning, Marcy went to collect Charlotte from her crib, and Charlotte was no longer breathing. She was only two and a half.

I have witnessed Marcy's heart break, unfortunately on too many occasions. But this heartbreak was different from the others. It wasn't like the loss of elders, or the end of relationships, or even the fear for one's own life. When I talked to Marcy on the phone that day, I heard her voice come from a deep and tortured place. She asked me, "Why would God give me this little girl, and then take her away like this? Why me? Why, after everything…?"

And I said this to her. I believed it then and I believe it now. "Some of us are warriors, and little Charlotte needed a warrior. If someone else, someone without your strength, had taken her, this would have been the end of that person. But you, you were not afraid of what was happening with her. You could be there, right along with her. You are made of steel. You are made of love."

To be fair, she didn't face this alone. Just as her father and sisters helped her to live through cancer, Lou helped her to live through this. And she helped him right back.

The story behind this love letter of a book has been clearly laid out by a woman who is made of both steel and love. She loved the fabulous Max and the complicated Charlotte, her

No one ever questions Marcy's resiliency, but just to prove a point: Here she is, shooting Ginger Cake right after Hurricane Dorian. Two feet of water had just receded from the room; the larder, vintage furniture, and brick chimney in the book's photos all had been lost. She hadn't even finished mopping…but she was baking. And photographing.

mother. But she also has both embraced and discovered her past. Her lineage. She has "gone down the middle of it." I remember when she first recognized her Jewish roots—a heritage that was held back from her because her family was scared to death. She literally saw herself differently from that day onward, curiously touching her curly hair, staring at her features in the mirror. It was as if she recognized herself for the first time. And that moment of truth, that moment of change, that moment of acceptance, happened when she was in her mid-fifties. Who knows what other life-changing revelations are in her future?

The story behind this love letter is the experience of a person who has gone down the middle of many difficult things. She has walked confidently down the center line. She has seen the other side. When she travels there again, she'll be fine with it, but she's enjoying today, on planet Earth. She comes from sturdy people who also saw the other side—and they kept baking. They kept singing, and swinging their hips, and playing cards…and whistling. And baking.

The very idea that Marcy keeps telling me that she's not "really a baker" is amusing. Perhaps not every cake comes out perfectly, like Max's. But she's captured the Brenner's Bakery flavors. She translated the recipes. She's brought the bakery back to life. And she's done much more than that. When she asked for my help, I guess I expected "just" a cookbook. I did not anticipate what Marcy was serving up.

EPILOGUE

There was a period in her early twenties when Marcy secretly wanted to take over the bakery, but Max always discouraged her. "You don't want to be a baker," he said. "The bakery is a nasty man's world, Baby. Long, hard hours on your feet, trying to find bakers who show up, pleasing customers, quality control, making payroll—it's a hard way to go."

But she was studying marketing, and she had big ideas. To combat the box stores and chain groceries with their "one-stop shopping" and in-house bakeries, she imagined telling the romantic story of an immigrant family, the recipes, and the nostalgia. She thought that when a customer would buy something from Brenner's, that item would come with a piece of the story—a piece of Max. She drew a logo of her grandfather in a horse and buggy, delivering bread and rolls. She imagined dressing up "the-ladies-in-the-front" in Old World dresses, putting lace curtains on the windows, and old sepia family photographs on the walls.

Right: An artist's rendering of Marcy's inspirational heritage graphic—the one that kept this book concept alive for the years it took to percolate.
Opposite page: Marcy on a "bucket list" trip to Paris in 2001, after her stem-cell transplant.

A BAKER'S DAUGHTER

Instead, she went on a road trip to California, roomed with my dad for a few months until she found a place—and then stayed for twenty years. There, she found the other side of herself and has been making music, in one way or another, ever since.

This love letter of a book is about every family and every journey. It just happens to have been written by a songwriter-baker and her friend—the friend who watched one of the strongest people she knows, being strong. Again and again, for a long time. And Marcy is not always on the receiving end. She's done the same for me, too.

What I loved most about this process was watching Marcy melt a little bit. I loved hearing her voice catch, or seeing photos of an imperfect cake she'd just pulled from the oven. I loved reading fresh lyrics, and listening to some new songs. It reminded me of when she visited me at college, and we hung around with her guitar or walked on the beach. It reminded me of the days before she faced the music.

This book is about feeding the spirit—most of all, hers. I loved watching Marcy bare her soul in a way that she didn't have to, with life and death. I hope her story is as delicious for you.

EPILOGUE

ACKNOWLEDGMENTS

Books are labors of love that require more than a strong sense memory about a Chocolate Top Cookie. This one was made with the support, enthusiasm, and contributions of friends and loved ones—all of whom said "yes," in honor of Max.

THANKS FROM MARCY

René Louis Castro, my best recipe sampler and my partner in all things. It's you and me, babe.

Sadie Weiss Brenner, my milk and honey; and Louis Brenner, my bread and water. Thank you for your bravery and your commitment to life and family.

Max and Charlotte Brenner, for making my family.

Linda Brenner, for your graceful, loving strength.

Judi Brenner Coyne, for protecting me and answering all of my questions.

Barbara Thompson Brenner, for loving Max. For bringing him so much ease and happiness in his life's long last chapter.

Christine Sherman, for testing the first converted recipes and sharing the exciting successes.

Jason Sherman, for remembering elusive details of finishing, and for giving me a glimpse of the baker's life "in the back."

Harry Sherman, for saving the handwritten ingredient cards, helping decode mysteries in the recipes, being a big brother, and mostly, for taking over the bakery—so I didn't have to.

Uncle Freddie, for being an example of living a life of curiosity and learning. For always encouraging music, reading and spiritual exploration. And for submitting to my interviews, providing an invaluable source of family information and stories.

Cousins, your Uncle Max loved you:

Joe Brenner, for calling me out of the blue to inform me that I was not Austrian, as our family lore had perpetuated, but that I was Polish. Pop was Polish.

Louis Brenner, for helping me to cross the bridge from the present to the past.

Stanley Metelits, for the treasure trove of photos and documents. Your mom Florence was one of the dearest persons I've ever known. She had the milk and honey, too.

Arlene Brenner, for fireflies (or is it lightning bugs?).

Elizabeth "Betsey" Brenner, for helping with genealogical pieces, and for sharing the details of her journey to Poland.

Janet Brown, for love, pictures, and memories.

Bob Baker, for finding me on ancestry.com and connecting me to Louis Brenner.

The Brenner family members who bravely reached America and brought the bakery with them, paving the way for us all.

And to Brenners who perished in the Holocaust. I have your names and I remember you.

My childhood friends: Alison Thompson Mandley, Mimi Brennan, and Eileen Keating Carnaggio (and the Bush Hill gang). Thanks for loving me—and not just my dad, the baker.

The Van Scoyocs, for letting me get dirty, watch rockets, and listen to Paul Harvey. And for the sheer joy of making music.

Karen Jones, for the coaching, cheerleading, inspiration—nd for providing an example of a working writer.

Susan Stuck, for that initial, inspiring—and intimidating—consultation about food writing, which spurred me on.

Danielle, for bread love, the stainless scraper, and patient photo staging.

Word Play Gathering folks: Pat Garber, Ruth Fordon, Ken DeBarth, Art Mines, Kelley Shinn, Peter Vankevich, Ginny Foard, Leslie Siddeley, Mitzi Crall, Stacy Huggins, Ava Carnaggio, Jen Grossi, and others. You inspire me.

Donald Davis and his workshop storytellers, for sharing the gift of story.

Laura Benassi Manning, for childhood memories, cake consulting, and recipe testing.

Lauren Strohl, for making the layer and pound cake I used for the photo shoot of Boston Cream Pie, Seven-Layer Cake and Petit Fours. Couldn't have made the deadline without you.

Mickey and George Roberson, for trading eggs for samples.

Every employee of the bakery through the decades, both guys and gals. Max loved you and appreciated you.

The Bakery's greater community and surrounding neighborhood, for the memories and the patronage.

The shop owners through the years at Belle View Shopping Center. They watched out for one another.

Facebook group, *Brenner's Bakery Memories*, for stories, recipe testing, moral support, encouragement, patience, love for the bakery and Max, and providing pieces to the puzzle.

Markos Panas (and his Dad), for continuing the tradition in his own way at the old bakery location.

Donna Glee, for recommending me for the Hambidge Creative Residency Program.

The Hambidge Center, for the Fellowship that gave me the space to conceive this book.

Judy and Doug Eifert of Dajio Restaurant, for freezer use that supported my photo shoots.

Party Time Chocolate Fudge Base, for making the perfect fudge base in the right quantity.

King Arthur Flour, for generous permission to reprint the sour starter recipes.

Ocracoke Preservation Society, for use of their scanner to duplicate photographs.

Jessie Morrissey and Shane Moore, for gorgeous photos.

Ginny Foard, for the illustrations that contributed a spark to every page.

Rockin' Dog Studios, for the killer design work. And John Edwards, for design consultation.

THANKS FROM KRISTIN

To the clan, past and present, who helped Marcy to live—and to bring her story to life.

My mom, Marcia Mitchell, the best writing champion ever.

Sara Bernstein, for a calm, warm, and true eye—even at the last minute. So far, each and every time.

And to our dads, both Max and Jack, the first men who glimpsed our natures—and told us that we would be okay, no matter what.

HITPA'EL
TO STUDY, TO TEACH ONES SELF

APPENDIX
BAKING NOTES

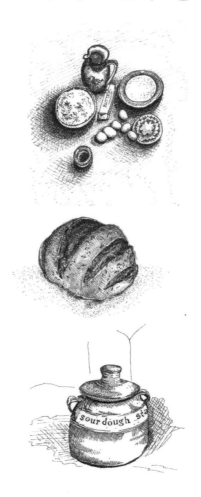

Before starting this project, I had baked cookies approximately 3,000 times in my own kitchen, but bread only a handful of times. I'd made pumpkin pies at Thanksgiving, cookies at Christmas, and a heart-shaped cake for Valentine's Day. But when it came to stepping back in time—and into the bakery—I had very few "breadcrumbs" to help me. In order to recreate the foods I'd grown up with, I had to bring Dad's list of ingredients to life. I hoped I would be able to recall how the dough looked, smelled, felt, and tasted. I hoped I could sense how it should act when mixing, when baking, or when it was warm out of the oven, or cool, or the next day.

    I picked up Dad's handwritten cards and the notes I'd taken. I did a bunch of math, and then…I'll admit: I didn't know if I could do it. I didn't know if successfully recreating Brenner's would first of all be possible—and if it was, if doing it would be experiential. That is, would baking be something I could teach myself, or was it something I would "remember," from my years in the bakery? Or maybe, just maybe, would it simply be a factor of my genes? Was being a Brenner enough?

    I shook off all of that and just stood at my counter as if it were the double-sided bakery work bench. I placed the ingredients and tools down the middle, like the bakers had always done. As I measured and stirred and folded, I could hear their stories, their dirty jokes, and their laughter. And it happened. I was right back there. I didn't know if it was memory or magic. And I didn't care.

My first approach was to try the recipes straight, no questions asked, no matter how weird any aspect might seem. But I didn't do it alone. My niece Christine, who spent many years at the front bakery counter, was a great help. She took my raw calculations and baked them up in tandem with me. We compared notes, mistakes, triumphs, and near misses. Her brother, Jason, had worked in the back of the bakery, and he was indispensable in confirming many of the finishing techniques. I also talked to baking friends, watched videos, read blogs, and even had a few "sessions" with a local bread master.

Before writing, I baked each of the fifty-plus recipes a minimum of three times. I made small changes, tried again, and fed lots of samples to my husband and neighbors.

APPENDIX

TAKING THE LEAP FROM BAKERY-KITCHEN TO HOME-KITCHEN

After my trial-and-error process, I ended up with lots of baking details. Therefore, I built this portion of the Appendix as a reference section. It includes what I learned about making recipes work in a non-industrial kitchen, as well as specific tips and techniques—both on how Brenner's Bakery did things and also on managing specific categories of recipes, from savory to sweet.

Even if you're a seasoned baker, I recommend that you read this section before getting elbow-deep in any recipe. Brenner's-specific tips really can make a difference—especially for Brenner's fans who know what you're looking for. And if you're not a seasoned baker, then you can take the trip along with me.

MODIFICATIONS

Throughout the book's recipes, I found elements that needed modification, such as commercial bakery techniques that didn't translate well to a home kitchen. When this happened, I took a moment to consider what home bakers are used to, and thought about accommodations. For example, most of the bakery's cookie recipes suggested shaping dough into logs and then slicing it. Home bakers, however, usually roll dough into balls, so that's how the recipes read here.

Other discoveries were hands-on gems, such as secrets that were missing from Dad's recipe notes, parts he'd kept in his head and his fingers. As it turned out, I found a little something special in almost every recipe—a small thing that made it "Brenner's." I made sure to keep track of every "secret code" that I cracked in my kitchen—and I sprinkled them throughout the book.

I also learned many larger-scale, hidden details that steered my overall bakery process. These fell into their own category—a "Baking Notes" reference section, which became a separate Appendix. The Appendix starts with a section called Ingredient Details (below), which describes unusual aspects of specific ingredients, or why they were chosen or suggested—either by my ancestors or by me. Ingredients are followed by a series of specialty sections that cover a range of topics: General Techniques (page 259), Cookie Techniques (page 263), Cake Techniques (page 264), and Bread Notes (page 267).

The Bread Notes section came about because I discovered very specific details that taught me how to be a better bread baker. In that section, you'll also find recipes and tips about making and using bread sours. If you've already got your own sours, you'll still find some tips relevant to these recipes.

INGREDIENT DETAILS

The bakery recipes revealed helpful details about how to manage ingredients. Those are included here. However, ingredients also provided unexpected clues that spurred my journey into family history—and you'll see those unfold throughout the book.

When my grandfather, Max's dad, said that "bread is the meaning of life," he was referring to white bread. At right is Max's recipe card for Brenner's version of this foundational staple. The card shows the bakery's pounds/ounces measurements used for large quantities—as well as one example of a common abbreviation. "MFB" stood for "Made For Baking" Shortening, made by Wesson.

FLOUR

All of the Brenner's Bakery ingredient cards list either cake, bread, whole wheat, or rye/pumpernickel flours. I always started with whatever was listed—but sometimes I ran into road blocks. For instance, cookie ingredient cards often called for cake flour, but cake flour is not available where I live.

Therefore, I began conducting some experiments—I tested some cookies with both cake and all-purpose flour. In practice, my results showed that in all circumstances—cookies and otherwise—these two different flours created only small differences. In cookies, I found that cake flour tends to produce a more delicate texture—but, perhaps surprisingly, I favored all-purpose. With cake flour, cookies are sublime, but almost too delicate. Too heavenly. I also like using all-purpose flour when

> WHITE BREAD
> 1 GAL WATER
> 0-3 YEAST
> 0-4 SALT
> 0-12 SUGAR
> 1-0 MILK P.
> 1-0 MFB
> 14-0 BREAD FLOUR

I can, because it's readily available in large quantities, in both unbleached and organic varieties.

In the end, I wrote the recipes so that you'll never wonder which flour to use. If a particular flour is listed, then my testing supported the bakery's instructions—and that's the best flour for that recipe. In all other cases, either cake or all-purpose flour will work just fine. Basically, you can decide how heavenly you want to get. I also learned something new: "All-purpose" was written on Dad's cards as "half bread" and "half cake"—which, I have come to find out, is the recipe for all-purpose flour.

EGGS

Figuring eggs was especially interesting. The bakery had big containers of whole, mixed eggs, as well as separated egg whites—making it a challenge to convert 3 pounds, 8 ounces (3-8) of eggs, or 2 quarts of egg whites, to a kitchen-sized recipe's "number of eggs." I had to learn how eggs effect a recipe in terms of texture, color, and taste, and eventually found a calculation that worked across all of the recipes.

For the record: In this book's recipes, "shortening" always refers to vegetable shortening, and "baking powder" means double-acting baking powder.

FAT

All of the Brenner's recipes call for shortening. At one point in the testing process, I decided to try butter in at least a few recipes in each category, just to see if was better than shortening. The thought of all that shortening seemed so...greasy. I was surprised

to learn that while the flavor with butter was great (but not better), the recipes didn't work. Butter has too much water, and recipes spread too much. To confirm, I expanded my trials, using butter with additional recipes from all of the categories. I also played with flour and water content—but then I heard my own advice, "Stay true to the recipes and trust them." Therefore, you'll see butter listed only as an occasional alternative, and no lard anywhere. Once I stopped questioning it, they all began working and coming out just like Brenner's.

The only hard and fast exception in the shortening rule was with pastry, where the bakery used "oleo"—what we call margarine today—in place of butter. It is a processed butter substitute made with vegetable oil. My first guess was that they used margarine because it was cheaper than butter. My second guess involved longevity; I had forgotten that a Brenner's Bakery cookie was even better the second day. When I used butter, it deteriorated quickly and was best the same day it was baked. However, in recipes with "oleo" or shortening the items held up better on the second day, and even the third.

Source for Fudge Base
Party Time
3350 Bluebonnet Blvd.,
Baton Rouge, LA 70809
(225) 927-3270
partytimebr.com, or
contact@partytimebr.com

FUDGE BASE

If you want to make your own fudge base, there are many recipes available online. However, I get mine from a company that has been making it for more than 40 years (see note). This base makes icing and glaze taste just like Brenner's. Tell them I sent you!

GENERAL TECHNIQUES

This section is not meant to be exhaustive; it's a collection of observations I made when making the recipes that made the cut.

THE KITCHEN ENVIRONMENT

In my kitchen, humidity and temperature changes impact baking, so the same recipe might be slightly different from day to day, or from season to season. This might be true for you, too.

The information in this volume has been recorded for the Outer Banks of North Carolina, averaged throughout the year. So it's relatively humid, and obviously low-lying. If you're high and dry, adjust according. I suggest that everyone look at and feel dough and batter—and then adjust accordingly for optimal liquid levels, as well as mixing/proofing/baking times.

TEMPERATURES

For all recipes, bring ingredients to room temperature before using, unless specifically noted otherwise. All oven, water, and product temperatures are listed in degrees Fahrenheit (°F).

TRANSLATING PAN SIZES

#1 Loaf Pan = 8½" x 4½"
Half Sheet = 13" x 18"
Pie Pan = 9"

APPENDIX

MANAGING THE OVEN

No matter how tempted you are, **don't open the oven** while something is baking. It's so hard, especially if there's no glass window on the oven door, like mine! But seriously. Don't do it. Also, **don't under bake.** Be sure to bake things until good-and-golden to deeply-golden brown. Don't fall into my bad habit; I tend not allow things to brown nicely, because I'm impatient.

INTERPRETING THE RECIPES / HANDLING INGREDIENTS AND DOUGH

In reinterpreting the recipes, "sticking with the ingredients cards" meant two things. After my experiments, I learned to remain faithful to the ingredients lists—including resisting adding extra flour when dough seemed sticky. I also learned to avoid overworking anything; no over-kneading bread dough or over-beating cake batters.

You can double or triple any of these recipes and they'll work, always keeping in mind that temperature and humidity, among other factors, change how things come out. Just be sure to feel your way through, and adjust as you go with flour and liquid.

MEASURING

Dad's handwritten lists of abbreviated ingredients were recorded in pounds-to-ounces ratios. After decoding everything with my family, I was able to translate measurements to basic

For the record:
There are 3 teaspoons in 1 tablespoon. This translates to:
2½ tablespoons (written "2½ T") = 2T + 1½ t, or 7½ t. Also, 2 tablespoons (written "2 T") = ⅛ cup.

home economics techniques. Here, you can measure ingredients by volume: cups (c), tablespoons (T), and teaspoons (t).

Flour and Powdered/Granulated Dry Ingredients

To measure flour, I find it best to fluff it in its container, gently fill the measuring cup until it's overflowing, then level off the top with a flat edge like a butter knife. If the recipe calls for sifting, measure then sift. This same principle applies to other dry ingredients, including granulated and powdered sugar, baking powder and soda, salt, milk powder, and spices.

Nuts and Other Dry Ingredients

Ingredients such as brown sugar, raisins, coconut, and nuts all should be firmly packed. However, anything chopped or processed—such as nuts or raisins—have to be chopped first, and then measured.

Fat/Shortening

Firmly pack, ensuring that air pockets are removed by pressing down as you fill shortenting to overflowing. Use a knife to level off.

FINISHING

Most of what the finished product looks like is in how it's "finished." An experienced baker will be a better "finisher" than a novice, whether shaping, cutting, placing, or scoring. I soon

realized that the most important goals are taste and texture; I tried to allow the look to develop organically as I went along. In specific recipes, I do my best to describe how to achieve the finish, but don't worry. Mine didn't look right at first, either. Fortunately, though, things did *taste* just like Brenner's.

PIPING DOUGH OR ICING

Some recipes in the book call for piping—especially selected cookie doughs, Éclair batter, and icings. If you don't have a pastry bag, then you can make one out of a plastic bag. Here's how: Hold the bag in one hand (or stuff it into a tall glass) and spoon the batter or icing into the bag, pushing it down to the bottom of the bag. Fold, roll, or twist the large opening of the bag, letting all the air escape. Then cut off one of the corners, making a hole about ¾ inches in diameter.

You can also make a decorating cone from parchment paper, which can be rolled into a wide funnel with a point. Fill it with dough or icing, and fold/roll/twist the large opening at the top to close, letting all the air escape. Then clip the tip into a plain round opening or a star shape, by cutting a zig-zag shape.

Refrigerate pastry bags or decorating cones in a plastic bag. When it's time to use them, simply heat or loosen the dough or icing with your hands before using. (Dad kept a whole selection of parchment icing cones—light blue, pink, yellow, green—all over the cake-decorating table.)

COOKIE TECHNIQUES

WHAT TO DO WHEN COOKIE DOUGH LOOKS "CURDLED"

When mixing the first few ingredients for cookie dough, they might not cream together properly. This happens especially if either the ingredients are cool, or your kitchen is cool. For a desperate moment, the dough might look curdled or separated. Fortunately, this is not the same as *being* curdled, and there's a quick cure. Just put the mixing bowl into another mixing bowl—one with a couple of inches of hot tap water in it—to warm the batter. This will allow it to cream together more easily.

P.S.: Don't tell anyone, but even if the batter still looks a bit curdled, it will mix and bake fine. So, if you're short on time, you can just keep going along without "curing the problem" at all.

SHAPING COOKIES

Most of the Brenner's cookies were mixed, made into a log, and cut. Some were piped. This was done for speed and efficiency, and is not the typical way a kitchen-baker finishes cookies. I tried them both ways—dropping by hand or with a spoon, as compared with cutting or piping—and found no practical difference.

Therefore, for the recipes, I standardized them so that bakers can either make balls of dough or roll out and cut, with the exception of Icebox Cookies. They are made in a spiral, so they have to be made into a log and then cut.

LIFTING COOKIES WITHOUT BREAKING

To lift a cookie from the cookie sheet without breaking it, I rely on two things. First, cooling; by allowing the cookie to set up some, it's less delicate and bendy. Second, the real secret is in the wrist. Even with a Gingerbread Person, you can release the cookie from the sheet—without its losing a limb—by employing a gentle twist. This is a hands-on technique (no spatula needed.) Try it!

CAKE TECHNIQUES

Cake recipes are relatively straightforward, but there's one task that can present a challenge.

CUTTING CAKE LAYERS HORIZONTALLY

Two items in this book require cutting layers into thinner horizontal layers—the Seven-Layer Cake and Petit Fours. I've discovered a few methods that can make this entire process easier, as it's awful when the cake falls apart. Everyone also hates cutting crooked layers.

Cutting Tools

Many people simply use a sharp, serrated knife that is longer than the layer. This usually cruises through the cake. Another cutting tool is dental floss, which can be pressed around the layer at the mid-line, all the way around the layer. Gently pull both ends over and beyond the other to cut the layer in half. Use a knife or spatula to gently lift the layer off. There's also a fancy, wire, cake-slicing gizmo, officially named a "cake leveler." I bought one (below), and it works great.

Special Techniques

You can try freezing the cake first, which keeps it sturdier while cutting. Many people find that it helps to mark each layer's "equator" by scoring with a paring knife or dotting toothpicks; use marks or toothpicks as a guide to keep the cuts straight.

BREAD NOTES

In general, the basic yeast bread process is: mix and proof (rise); then fold, shape, proof; then egg-wash and score; then bake. That's the order of things. These tips fall into that order.

MIXING THE DOUGH—DON'T OVERWORK IT!

The general approach to the yeast recipes is that less is more. They don't need to be worked that much. They also don't need too much added flour. Let the dough be sticky and wet for the first rise. It makes for a moist bread like the Bakery's. The less I did, the better everything came out. Don't overthink it, and definitely don't think that because you are not a baker, or you are afraid of yeast, you can't make these recipes. You can!

BE GENTLE

This dough is precious. Gently turn it out into the prepared bowl or lightly floured work surface or board, then "fold and pat." Please don't punch it, ever. I like to say, "no dough was harmed in making these recipes."

TRUST THE RECIPE—AND YOUR HANDS

Some of these doughs are very wet and sticky after mixing, before the first rise. You might feel an initial impulse to add flour. Resist, because often after the first rise, the dough is no longer wet and becomes luscious when you fold and shape the bread or

rolls. Therefore, let the dough have a moment. Then, add flour after the first rise if your hands tell you to; add moisture if they say so. Do these in small amounts at a time. Keep in mind that you're feeling more than flour and water; humidity, temperature, altitude, how gluten contracts and relaxes, and yeast spores in your kitchen all affect how dough feels and reacts.

In perfecting the bread recipes in your kitchen, I suggest that you first make the recipe as is and see how it reacts in your kitchen, then add or subtract liquid and/or flour accordingly. If I have to change anything, I find it best to first alter the water amount while keeping the flour amount as indicated. You also might try saving out ⅓-cup of the water and adding it as the dough goes through the long knead, adding small amounts until arriving at the texture/moisture you want. These are fine points, and experimenting will make a recipe your own. However, each recipe should come out great just straight out of the book, even considering slight variations in environment.

FLOURED HANDS AND SURFACE

When shaping bread, one mission is to avoid accidentally drying out your bread. Therefore, allow sticky dough to remain sticky, and then use floured hands and a very lightly floured surface when handling. This prevents the dough from sticking to your hands or your work surface. The floured surface also provides some friction that makes it easier to shape your loaves.

HUMIDITY AND TEMPERATURE

Hot tap water is typically 105 to 110 degrees Fahrenheit. Both water and flour might need to be adjusted slightly due to humidity, temperature, and altitude. In general, you know whether you need more or less water or flour when, during the first mix, the dough is way too sticky or way too dry. To know what temperature the hot water is, I have used a candy thermometer, but a digital thermometer is better. And a digital thermometer can be used to check the bake.

FIRST KNEAD & SCRAPER/HAND METHOD

Some of the yeast recipes produce dough that is rather wet. It still comes away from the dough hook when ready, but it won't necessarily come away from the sides of the bowl and will need to be scraped out. Resist the urge to add flour.

You can use either a standing mixer or your hands. If you mix by hand, I recommend using one hand; in the other, use a scraper or spatula. Knead by scraping, folding, and pressing. When kneading by hand, you'll want to knead for about twice as long.

PROOFING DOUGH ("RISING")

Professionals use the word "proof," but home bakers usually say "rise." No matter what you call it, prepare a large glass bowl by lightly oiling with spray or vegetable shortening. Prepare a warm proofing spot (70-90°F); the microwave or oven with the light on

is a great proof box for containers; for larger pans, the oven works (but don't turn it on!). While you're preparing the dough, also prepare the proofing spot with a glass measuring cup filled with boiling water, which provides both humidity and warmth. Then, pop the dough into its warming spot to rise. Refresh the hot water as many times as needed to maintain the desired proofing temperature. The perfect temperature in my kitchen is 80°F.

PLASTIC VERSUS CLOTH PROOFING COVERS

I prefer floured or oiled plastic to cover rising dough. It doesn't stick and it keeps the dough moist and warm. My favorite is an oversized food-storage bag—cut open along the sides and minus the "zipper." It's thicker plastic than plastic wrap and stands up and off the dough, making a folded dome of plastic that covers most large bowls and allows for plenty of rise.

I've found that using a cloth is potentially troublesome, especially on the second rise. If the cloth sticks, then it pulls on the dough, both ruining its beautiful shape and making it fall.

Another good option is a floured or oiled plastic bowl cover, the kind with elastic that looks like a shower cap from a hotel. In fact, a shower cap from a hotel works great.

TIMING THE RISE

When talking about the timing of any rise, I find it works best to pay more attention to what the dough is doing in the kitchen and less about the amount of elapsed time. There are many factors that affect rising time, so it's better to use your eyes and hands rather than the clock to determine when the rise is done.

If dough is over-proofed at any stage, it will rise and then fall before you get it baked. This is especially true for the final rise. If you let it proof too long, then the bread will collapse under the crust in the oven. I've learned that if I go for just "a little more rise," then it falls.

First Rise/Proof
Generally, for the first rise, you want the dough to be full and puffy, but not quite double in size.

Last (Second) Rise/Proof
For the second (last) rise—whether in the pan or on the sheet:

The **baking sheet loaf** will not double in size. When a floured finger pokes into the side, the "dimple" doesn't immediately fill back in. The dough doesn't have any rise left. You'll see that technique called the Dimple Test in the text.

The **loaf pan dough** should be a round dome with the dough expanded out to fill the pan, but without a "muffin top" effect of oozing up and over the sides. The rule of thumb is to use the Dimple Test, and also let it rise to the level of "one thumb, to the first knuckle" above the top edge of the bread pan.

Rolls will be puffy, but not double in size.

DOUGH HAS MEMORY

Yeast dough has a "memory." Do each step as best you can and go with how it comes out. Once you shape bread dough, it will "remember" what you did and fight if you try to change it. If it feels like the dough is fighting when you begin to work with it, then put it in "time out."

The Brenners used the term "bench rest," which meant to roll it into a ball, cover with floured plastic, and let it rest for 10 minutes. This allows the gluten fibers to relax. After the 10 minutes have passed, pick it up where you left off, and the dough should let you shape it.

No matter what, you don't want to overwork your dough. So, in the worst case, if the shape isn't what you hoped for, just live with the shape it becomes. It'll still taste great!

FOLDING

Fold the top of the dough toward you, gently press down, and then gently pat to get any gas bubbles out. Fold the left side in, the right side in, and press and pat. Fold the top half toward you, press and pat.

SHAPING BREAD AND ROLLS

There is an artistry to shaping the dozens of varieties of breads and rolls that are baked in loaves and on sheet pans. With practice, these become second-nature.

King Arthur has great blogs about bread dough techniques. Look for blogs on shaping, scoring, and others. It might help to see these in action at kingarthurflour.com.

Pan Loaves

Divide dough in half. Fold each segment, roll/tuck into a loaf shape, and set into a prepared loaf pan (two loaves per recipe).

Rolls

Fold dough. Cut into equal bits, about 24 rolls per recipe. Place each bit on your surface and roll it around loosely under your palm and fingers to form a smooth ball. Pinch under to tighten the top, and place rolls 2" apart on prepared baking sheets.

Baking Sheet Loaves (like Brenner's)

Divide dough in half (or, for baguettes, into quarters). Fold each segment, and then form into a ball, bâtard, or baguette shape. (Shapes are described below.) Place on a prepared baking sheet. Leave at least four inches between the loaves so they won't touch during the baking process. You can also use a dusting of cornmeal on the sheet, which keeps dough from sticking and also creates a nice effect on your finished bread.

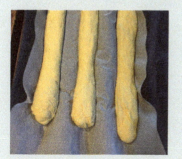

Shapes

A **"baguette"** is a long, narrow loaf. Make this shape by rolling a section of dough under floured palms, pressing the dough out as your roll it into a long log. I then place a parchment-covered towel on a baking sheet, and place the rolled dough onto the parchment, pushing the towel on each side to make a "trough"

to hold each baguette's shape during the final rise. If the towel slips, you can use clothes pins to hold it together.

A "**boule**" shape is round. Create a round "bubble" of dough. With floured hands, roll it on a very lightly floured surface, letting the ball roll around under your palms and fingers, which hover on the work surface. Then pinch each roll underneath and tuck the edges under to form little tight ball. (This is same technique for making round rolls, with smaller sections of dough.)

A "**bâtard**" shape is like a football, shorter and fatter than a baguette; it comes to a round point on each end. Make a "boule" and then allow it to lengthen and narrow at the ends. Tuck under the seam (which remains underneath, from folding), and pinch down the ends.

The Big Finish

A final shaping technique requires a great deal of finesse and practice, and has been perfected by my "bread fairy," Danielle. This final touch involves stretching the "skin" of the dough while the dough is in contact with the table. Danielle's method is to place both hands on the dough, with heels of the hands at opposite ends (elbows pointing out), fingertips pointing toward one another. With thumbs and pinky fingers doing most of the stretching of the dough surface, the bread "shuffles" or slightly rolls toward and then away, over and over. In the process, the dough slightly turns under your fingers. The bread will be fine without this last maneuver, but stretching makes for a wonderful crust, consistent oven rise, and generally a fine loaf of bread.

SCORING

Scoring, or slashing, a loaf of bread creates a visually pleasing pattern—and it helps control the expansion of the loaf as it bakes, by giving the rising dough a path for expansion. Breads in loaf pans are typically not scored. Breads on a baking sheet typically are scored, although Brenner's instead "punched" the Rye and Pumpernickel breads. As mentioned earlier, this is not an act of violence, but instead a slicing of several three-inch-deep holes with a lame (pronounced "lahm," sounds like "mom"), a razor blade on a stick with a handle. I've even used the digital thermometer to punch holes in my Rye and Pumpernickel loaves.

If you prefer to use the lame to score (instead of punch) the bread, then cut quickly and with the corner of the blade, ¼-inch deep, at a 30-degree angle. You also can use a very sharp knife, in a very quick ¼-inch cut, to achieve similar results without a lame. No matter what, you don't want to deflate your beautiful loaf, so score quickly and then pop it in the oven for the oven rise. If you want to top your bread (see below), then Egg Eash it (or spritz with water), score it, then top it, and bake.

The general pattern for scoring is one long, diagonal slash for a single loaf like a Rye or Pumpernickel. For a round "boule" loaf, cut three small diagonal slashes or a crisscross pattern.

TOPPING

You can top your breads, bagels, or rolls by using egg wash or spritzing with water, and then sprinkling with a topping, just before placing into the preheated oven. You might try sesame, caraway, sunflower, and poppy seeds.

Egg Wash: They used this egg wash for everything at Brenner's. It browns nicely and gives a beautiful shine.

    1 egg
    1 T water
    Pinch salt
    Whisk together, gently brush on dough before baking.

BAKING

Baking is done when the bread sounds hollow when gently tapped. It will also feel "lighter" when it has been baked enough. The temperature in the center should be about 195°F. Be patient here if you want a good crust and crumb; don't rush the ever-important baking process.

In a loaf pan or for rolls, if the top is deep brown, then the sides will be done, too. Did I mention? Don't under bake.

All of the yeast breads can be baked in a loaf pan for sliced "sandwich" bread. Rye, Pumpernickel, Marble Rye, French Bread, and Sourdough are typically baked on a sheet, but can also be baked in a loaf pan or as rolls.

Cooling

For baking sheet loaf, pan loaf, or rolls, place the baked bread in a spot away from the oven, on a cooling rack, so that air circulates all around it. Cool baking sheet breads and rolls on a rack right away. For loaf pan breads, allow to cool in the pan until it can be tilted out of the pan and onto a cooling rack without collapsing or crushing. If you leave it in the pan until fully cool, then the bread will sweat and the crust will become soft. If you take it out too soon, it will collapse in on itself. It's a Zen thing to know when.

Slicing

Do not slice your bread until fully cool or you'll collapse your beautiful loaf. We hate that.

MORE TIPS AND INFORMATION

King Arthur Flour Company

King Arthur Flour, among many other online sources, has videos demonstrating all aspects of bread making that are useful, especially with shaping. This is also my source for flour and most other baking ingredients. And they kindly granted me permission to reprint their Rye Sour and Sour Starter recipes in this book. Thanks, King Arthur! www.kingarthur.com.

BREAD SOURS

The world of sours is one of smells and tastes and textures like no other. They're not hard; they just require good, clean ingredients, proper conditions, time, and attention.

There was no ingredient card for "sour," which is in the sour dough and rye breads. In order to choose the best replacement, I apprenticed myself in bread "sours"—also known as "starters" and "mothers"—and settled on King Arthur Flour sour dough starter and rye sour. These recipes are reprinted (with quantities/temps as provided), with King Arthur's gracious permission.

Sourdough recipe
To begin:
1 c whole rye / pumpernickel flour (or whole wheat flour)
½ c cool water

To feed starter:
a scant 1 c all-purpose flour
½ c water
(cool if house is warm; lukewarm if house is cool)

SOURDOUGH STARTER

This is King Arthur Flour recipe #10009. This starter is essential for both Sourdough bread and also the Rye Sour, which appears on following pages.

Day 1: Combine the pumpernickel or whole wheat flour with the cool water in a non-reactive container. Glass, crockery, stainless steel, or food-grade plastic all work fine for this.

Stir everything together thoroughly; make sure there's no dry flour anywhere. Cover the container loosely and let the mixture sit at warm room temperature (about 70°F) for 24 hours. See tips on following pages for advice about growing starters in a cold house.

Day 2: You may see no activity at all in the first 24 hours, or you may see a bit of growth or bubbling. Either way, discard half the starter (4 ounces, about 1/2 cup), and add to the remainder a scant 1 cup King Arthur Unbleached All-Purpose Flour, and ½ cup cool water (if your house is warm); or lukewarm water (if it's cold).

Mix well, cover, and let the mixture rest at room temperature for 24 hours.

Day 3: By the third day, you'll likely see some activity—bubbling; a fresh, fruity aroma, and some evidence of expansion.

It's now time to begin two feedings daily, as evenly spaced as your schedule allows. For each feeding, weigh out 4 ounces starter; this will be a generous ½ cup, once it's thoroughly stirred down. Discard any remaining starter.

FEEDING: Add a scant 1 cup (4 ounces) King Arthur Unbleached All-Purpose Flour, and ½ cup water to the 4 ounces starter. Mix the starter, flour, and water, cover, and let the mixture rest at room temperature for approximately 12 hours before repeating.

Day 4: Weigh out 4 ounces starter and discard any remaining starter. Feed as above.

Day 5: Weigh out 4 ounces starter and discard any remaining starter. Feed as above.

By the end of Day 5, the starter should have at least doubled in volume. You'll see lots of bubbles, and perhaps some little "rivulets" on the surface, full of finer bubbles. Also, the starter should have a tangy aroma—pleasingly acidic, but not

overpowering. If your starter hasn't risen much and isn't showing lots of bubbles, then repeat discarding and feeding every 12 hours on Day 6, and, if necessary Day 7—as long as it takes to create a vigorous (risen, bubbly) starter. Note: More details about this process are listed in the Sours Tips later in this chapter.

Once the starter is ready, give it one last feeding. Discard all but 4 ounces (a generous ½ cup). Feed as usual. Let the starter rest at room temperature for 6 to 8 hours; it should be active, with bubbles breaking the surface. Hate discarding so much starter? See the Sours Tips on following pages.

Remove however much starter you need for your recipe (no more than 8 ounces, about 1 cup); and transfer the remaining 4 ounces of starter to its permanent home: a crock, jar, or whatever you'd like to store it in long-term. Feed this reserved starter with 1 cup of flour and ½ cup water, and let it rest at room temperature for several hours, to get going, before refrigerating it.

Maintenance: Store this starter in the refrigerator and feed it regularly; we recommend feeding it with a scant 1 cup flour and ½ cup water once a week.

RYE SOUR

There are two Rye Sour recipes, Quick and Long, and both come from King Arthur Flour. The Long recipe has more flavor.

Rye / quick recipe
1 rounded T (½ oz, 14 g) fed ("ripe") sourdough starter
2¼ c (8⅜ oz, 237 g) organic pumpernickel flour
⅞ c (7 oz, 198g) room temperature water (70°F)

Quick
Use this one if your priority is time; glance through the long one to see its benefits. Even this "short" one will require 13 to 16 hours before you can mix and bake your bread.

Note that the water temperature for this overnight sour is 70°F, as is the desired rising temperature. Water temperature and room temperature both play a key role in the proper fermentation of your rye sour, so it's beneficial to try to replicate these conditions as closely as you can.

This rye sour will be very thick, and a bit arduous to stir by hand. This is normal, allowing for a long, slow fermentation. You can also mix the sour in a stand mixer with the paddle attachment on the lowest speed, stirring just until all the flour is thoroughly moistened.

After mixing, place the rye sour in a non-reactive container with room to grow (it won't quite double, but needs some room for expansion). Smooth it out and sprinkle a small amount of pumpernickel flour on top, to cover the sour.

Why the sprinkling of pumpernickel? This is a traditional practice with rye starters, meant to protect the starter and also to make it easier to tell when the starter is fully ripened.

At full maturity, the sour will dome on top and show islands of rye flour surrounded by small cracks and crevices. It looks a little volcanic in nature. There'll be small bubbles visible from the side of the container and the sour will have risen up, although not quite doubled in size. This will take about 13 to 16 hours at 70°F.

Long
This recipe also requires Sourdough Starter (see notes below). The longer method is truly better for flavor. The flavor of the longer Rye Sour makes the bread taste just like Brenner's.

First feeding: Combine the ¼ cup starter (either unfed or received as a discard from someone else) with ¼ cup room-temperature water and a heaping ½ cup pumpernickel flour (organic preferred).

Rye / long recipe
To begin / first feeding:
¼ c sourdough starter, unfed/discard
¼ c water (room temperature, 70°F)
½ c (heaping) pumpernickel flour, organic

To feed starter:
¼ c starter from above
¼ c water (room-temperature, 70°F)
½ c (heaping) pumpernickel flour, organic

Place the starter in a nonreactive container. Sprinkle a light coating of pumpernickel flour over the top of the starter and cover it.

Allow the starter to rise for 12 hours at room temperature (70°F).

12 Hours Later (second feeding): Keep ¼ cup of your initial starter; discard or give away the rest. Feed the ¼ cup starter with ¼ cup room-temperature water and a heaping ½ cup pumpernickel flour.

Sprinkle the top of the starter with pumpernickel flour and cover it. Allow the starter to rise for 12 hours at room temperature.

Every 12+ Hours for a Few Days: Repeat feedings as above until the starter is rising well and has a pleasantly tangy odor. The more feedings you give it, the better, as it takes a few days for the starter to completely establish itself as a rye starter.

Maintenance: Once the starter is rising well, you can refrigerate it for up to a week before feeding it again. Feed your starter as above and allow it to sit out at room temperature for 2 hours before returning to the fridge.

Marble Rye Tip:
If making Marble Rye recipe (two 2# loaves) then double every measure in this Rye Sour starter recipe. You'll need 3⅓ c of Rye Sour for the Marble Rye recipe so plan your container for expansion. I use a 50-oz glass jar.

KING ARTHUR'S SOURS TIPS:

Temperature

If your rye starter has been stored in the refrigerator, then be sure to give it two or three feedings at room temperature (morning and evening) before you plan to use it in a recipe. This will revive it and help achieve optimum rise and flavor in your bread.

The colder the environment, the more slowly your starter will grow. If the normal temperature in your home is below 68°F, then I suggest finding a smaller, warmer spot to develop your starter. For instance, try setting the starter atop your water heater, refrigerator, or another appliance that might generate ambient heat. Your turned-off oven—with the light turned on—is also a good choice. [Marcy's note: In my house, the microwave with light on stays right at 70°F.]

Discarding Starter

Why do you need to discard half the starter? It seems so wasteful. Well, it's necessary for three reasons. First, unless you discard, eventually you'll end up with The Sourdough That Ate Milwaukee—just too much starter. Second, keeping the starter volume the same helps balance the pH. And third, keeping the volume down offers the yeast more food to eat each time you feed it; it's not fighting with quite so many other little yeast cells to get enough to eat. Also, you don't have to discard it if you don't want to; you can give it to a friend, or use it to bake. There are quite a few recipes on our website using "discard" starter, including sourdough pizza crust, sourdough pretzels, and…waffles.

The direct link to King Arthur Flour's sours recipes is: kingarthurflour.com/recipes/sourdough-starter-recipe

Timing

Add your rye starter to a recipe after it's been fed and isn't quite doubled in size. It will be domed on top, with islands of rye flour surrounded by cracks and crevices. This will likely take about 8 hours at 70°F, but everyone's starter will be a little different.

APPENDIX

One of the King Arthur site's readers offers the following thoughts about the duration of daily feedings, which I agree is great advice: "Conditions vary so widely that 7 days can be far too little. I've learned the key is to watch for a dramatic and consistent rise in the jar—at least doubling between 1 and 4 hours after feeding. This could be 7 days or less after you begin, or it could be three weeks (for me it was 12 to 14 days). I would encourage you to consider tweaking your wording a bit to guide bakers to watch for this phenomenon, rather than to watch the calendar."

Flour
You can substitute medium rye flour for pumpernickel, but pumpernickel flour is preferable. The starter will likely ferment more quickly with medium rye flour because it will be wetter.

Why start with whole-grain flour?
Because the wild yeast that gives sourdough starter its life is more likely to be found in the flora- and fauna-rich environment of a whole-grain flour than in all-purpose flour.

Should you use bottled water?
Unless your tap water is so heavily treated that you can smell the chemicals, there's no need to use bottled water; tap water is fine.

ILLUSTRATION CREDITS

Except where noted, all "people photos" from Brenner family collection; in-process baking/recipe snapshots by Marcy Brenner.

OTHER PHOTOGRAPHY
Ehringhaus, Ann: 288
Glock, Sylvie: 243
Langley, Jeff: 74 (Edison High School yearbook photo ad, posted on *brenner's bakery memories* Facebook page; shared by Jennifer L. Irvin)
Legg, Adrian: 238
Lovejoy, Karen: 183
Manning, Laura Benassi: 134
Morrissey, Jessie & Shane Moore, with styling by Danielle: 46, 70, 93, 118, 220, 226, 244, 286
Townsend, Steve: 167
Woolgar, Carol: 236

ILLUSTRATIONS
Ginny Foard

ABOUT THE AUTHORS

Marcy Brenner
With the fabulous Lou, in the beginning—of their marriage, and of Coyote, their musical collaboration. Here, they're "warming up" at the Ocracoke Community Center, 2003.

Marcy is a musician, songwriter, and cancer advocate. She balances a need for solitude with her joy in sharing music and serving others. She lives on Ocracoke Island, twenty miles from shore, with her husband Louis Castro—"Mr. Lou" to his music students—and 1,000 of their closest neighbors and friends. Like Marcy, her town is a quiet historic village for part of the year and a tourist mecca for the other. Her specialty is starting over.

As a cancer survivor and inspirational speaker, Marcy travels all over the country—sharing her message of prevailing, a backhanded gift that cancer bestowed on her. She "goes anywhere and does anything" to help others through their cancer journeys. A 2008 documentary film of her story, entitled *Dead Girl Walking*—made by Ray Schmitt of Real Earth Productions—won the Amazing Grace Award at Toronto's BreastFest Film Festival, among other honors at various festivals and events.

Together, Marcy and Lou have written, recorded, and published three original music CDs: *Home To Me*, *Another Year Blooms*, and *My Live Oak*. Since Hurricane Dorian flooded their historic live-music venue on the harbor, they are "bringing it home" to their living room. With true house concerts, they will help rebuild their village—and recreate their lives, once again.

Kristin Donnan
In a book-promotion shot with her mother, Marcia (above left), 1972. This was for "the other recipe book" in Krissy's life: *Cosmetics from the Kitchen,* Marcia's first book.

This book is about families. Krissy comes by her profession because she fledged from a family tree populated by writers, from both branches of the maternal line. Family genealogists have linked her great-great-grandfather, California historian Horace Sessions Foote, and his descendant Mark Foote, a journalist and Washington correspondent. On the other side is poet and great-grandmother Gertrude Alcott Shoemaker; Louisa May Alcott was related to her. And today, Krissy's mother, Marcia Mitchell, has written more than a dozen books, including *The Spy Who Tried to Stop a War,* which inspired 2019's *Official Secrets*—a true story of a British whistleblower, starring Keira Knightley. Krissy and her mom edit for each other. Fiercely and honestly.

Krissy has spent her adult life as a freelance writer, authoring or coauthoring several books—including *Rex Appeal*, the source material for the 2014 Emmy®-winning documentary *Dinosaur 13*, a film she assisted during production. She also writes, researches, and/or edits for other authors, as well as for television, film, and giant-screen projects. She's co-owned both an art magazine and a bronze foundry, and has received national and state writing awards. As of this writing, she has a tantalizing line-up of (patient) books and scripts on deck. She adores Chocolate Top Cookies.